Charlotte M. Yonge

John Keble's Parishes: A History Of Hursley And Otterbourne

© 2025, Charlotte M. Yonge (domaine public)
Édition : BoD - Books on Demand, 31 avenue Saint-Rémy,
57600 Forbach, bod@bod.fr
Impression : Libri Plureos GmbH, Friedensallee 273,
22763 Hamburg (Allemagne)
ISBN : 978-2-3225-5316-7
Dépôt légal : Avril 2025

John Keble's Parishes: A History Of Hursley And Otterbourne
By
Charlotte M. Yonge

John Keble's Parishes: A History Of Hursley And Otterbourne

CHAPTER I - MERDON AND OTTERBOURNE

The South Downs of England descend at about eight miles from the sea into beds of clay, diversified by gravel and sand, and with an upper deposit of peaty, boggy soil, all having been brought down by the rivers of which the Itchen and the Test remain.

On the western side of the Itchen, exactly at the border where the chalk gives way to the other deposits, lies the ground of which this memoir attempts to speak. It is uneven ground, varied by undulations, with gravelly hills, rising above valleys filled with clay, and both alike favourable to the growth of woods. Fossils of belemnite, cockles (cardium), and lamp-shells (terebratula) have been found in the chalk, and numerous echini, with the pentagon star on their base, are picked up in the gravels and called by the country people Shepherds' Crowns - or even fossil toads. Large boulder stones are also scattered about the country, exercising the minds of some observers, who saw in certain of them Druidical altars, with channels for the flow of the blood, while others discerned in these same grooves the scraping of the ice that brought them down in the Glacial age.

But we must pass the time when the zoophytes were at work on our chalk, when the lamp-shells rode at anchor on shallow waves, when the cockles sat "at their doors in a rainbow frill," and the belemnites spread their cuttlefish arms to the sea, and darkened the water for their enemies with their store of ink.

Nor can we dwell on the deer which left their bones and horns in the black, boggy soil near the river, for unfortunately these were disinterred before the time when diggers had learnt to preserve them for museums, and only reported that they had seen remains.

Of human times, a broken quern was brought to light when digging the foundation of Otterbourne Grange; and bits of pottery have come to light in various fields at Hursley, especially from the barrows on Cranbury Common. In 1882 and 1883 the Dowager Lady Heathcote, assisted by Captain John Thorp, began to search the barrows on the left hand side of the high road from Hursley to Southampton, and found all had been opened in the centre, but scarcely searched at all on the sides. In July they found four or five urns of unbaked clay in one barrow - of early British make, very coarse, all either full of black earth or calcined bones, and all inverted and very rough in material, with the exception of one which was of a finer material, red, and like a modern flower-pot in shape. Several of these urns were deposited in the Hartley Museum, Southampton.

Of the Roman times we know nothing but that part of the great Roman road between Caer Gwent (or Venta Belgarum, as the Romans called Winchester) and Sorbiodunum (Old Sarum). It can still be traced at Hursley, and fragments of another leading to Clausentum (Southampton) on the slope of Otterbourne hill.

In Dr. Milner's History of Winchester, written at the end of the last century, he describes a medallion of mixed metal bearing the head of Julius Cæsar, which was dug up by a labourer at Otterbourne, in the course of making a new road. He thought it one of the plates carried on the Roman standards of the maniples; but alas! on being sent, in 1891, to be inspected at the British Museum, it was pronounced to be one of a cinquecento series of the twelve Cæsars.

The masters of the world have left us few traces of their possession, and in fact the whole district was probably scarcely inhabited; but the trees and brushwood or heather of the southern country would have joined the chalk downs, making part of what the West Saxons called the Jotunwald, or Giant's Wood, and the river Ytene, and so Itchen seems to have been named in like manner.

These were the times when churches were built and the boundaries of estates became those of parishes. The manor of Merdon, which occupied the whole parish of Hursley, belonged to the Bishops of Winchester by a grant   of Oynegils, first Christian King. Milner, in his History of Winchester, wishes to bestow on Merdon the questionable honour of having been the place where, in the year 754, the West Saxon King Cenwulf was murdered by his brother in the house of his lady-love; but Mr. Marsh, the historian of Hursley, proves at some length that Merton in Surrey was more likely to have been the scene of the tragedy.

Church property being exempted from William the Conqueror's great survey, neither Merdon nor Hursley appears in Domesday Book, though Otterbourne, and even the hundred of Boyate or Boviate, as it is in the book, appear there. It had once belonged, as did Baddesley first, at first to one named Chepney, then to Roger de Mortimer, that fierce Norman warrior who was at first a friend and afterwards an enemy to William I.

The entire district, except the neighbourhood of Merdon Manor on the one hand, and of the Itchen on the other, was probably either forest ground or downs, but it escaped the being put under forest laws at the time when the district of Ytene became the New Forest. Probably the king was able to ride over down, heather, and wood, scarcely meeting an enclosure the whole way from Winchester; and we can understand his impatience of the squatters in the wilder parts, though the Cistercian Abbey of Beaulieu was yet to be founded. Indeed Professor E. A. Freeman does not accept the statement that there could possibly have been thirty-nine village churches to be destroyed in the whole district of "Ytene."

The tradition lingered to the present time at Otterbourne that the corpse of William Rufus was brought back in Purkiss's wood-cart from Minestead to Winchester for burial in the Cathedral, along a track leading from Hursley to Otterbourne, called at each end King's Lane, though it is not easy to see how the route could have lain through both points.

The parish of Hursley lies in the hundred of Buddlesgate, and division of Fawley; and the village is situated on the turnpike-road leading from Winchester to Romsey, and nearly at an equal distance from each of those places.

The parishes by which Hursley is surrounded were, when Mr. Marsh wrote, Sparsholt on the north; Farley on the north-west; Michelmersh and Romsey on the west; Baddesley, North Stoneham, and Otterbourne on the south; and Compton and St. Cross on the east.

The whole parish was then upwards of twenty-eight miles in circumference, and contained 10,590 acres of land, of which 2600 were in common, 372 in roads and lanes, about 1000 under growth of coppice-wood, and the rest either arable or pasture.

The soil in the parish of Hursley, as may be supposed in so extensive a tract of land, is of several different sorts; in some parts it is light and shallow, and of a chalky nature; in others, particularly on the east and west sides of the parish, it is what is called strong land, having clay for its basis; and in others, especially that of the commons and fields adjoining, it consists principally of sand or gravel. Towards the west, it is entirely covered with wood, not in general bearing trees of large size, but some beautiful beech-trees; and breaking into peaty, boggy ground on the southern side. The northern side is of good rich loam, favourable to the growth of fine trees, and likewise forms excellent arable land. This continues along the valley of Otterbourne, along a little brook which falls into the Itchen. It is for the most part of thick clay, fit for brick-making, with occasional veins of sand, and where Otterbourne hill rises, beds of gravel begin and extend to the borders of the Itchen, through a wooded slope known as Otterbourne Park.

The boundaries of estates fixed those of parishes, and Otterbourne was curiously long and narrow, touching on Compton and Twyford to the north and north-west, on Stoneham to the south, and Hursley to the west, lying along the bank of the Itchen.

The churches of both parishes were probably built in the twelfth century, for though Hursley Church has been twice, if not three times, rebuilt, remains of early Norman mouldings have been found built into the stone-work of the tower. And on the wall of the old Otterbourne Church a very rude fresco came partially to light. Traced in red was a quatrefoil within a square, the corners filled up with what had evidently been the four Cherubic figures, though only the Winged Ox was clearly traceable. Within the quatrefoil was a seated Figure, with something like scales in one hand, apparently representing our Lord in His glory. The central compartment was much broken away, but there was the outline of a man whom one in a hairy garment was apparently baptizing. The rest had disappeared.

These paintings surmounted three acutely-pointed arches, with small piers, and square on the side next the nave, but on the other side slender shafts with bell-shaped capitals, carved with bold round mouldings and deep hollows. Two corbels supporting the horizontal drip-stone over the west window were also clear and sharply cut; and the doorway on the south side had slender shafts and deep mouldings, in one of which is the dog-tooth moulding going even down to the ground on each side. This is still preserved in the entrance to the Boys' School.

These remnants date the original building for about the thirteenth century. It may have been due to King Stephen's brother, Bishop Henry de Blois of Winchester, who is known to have raised the castle whose remains still exist on his manor of Merdon, where once there had been a Roman encampment. So far as his work can be traced, the first thing he would do would be to have a similar embankment thrown up, and a parapet made along the top, behind which men-at-arms would be stationed, the ditch below having a stockade of sharp stakes. In the middle of the enclosure a well was begun, which had to go deeper and deeper through the chalk, till at last water was found at 300 feet deep - a work that must have lasted a year or more. Around the well, leaving only a small courtyard, were all the buildings of the castle meant for the Bishop's household and soldiers. The entrance to it all was probably over a drawbridge across the great ditch (which, on this side, was not less than 60 feet deep), and through a great gateway between two high square towers, which must have stood where now there is a slope leading down from the level of the inner court to that surrounded by a bank. This slope is probably formed by the ruins of the gateway and tower having been pitched into the ditch, as the readiest way of getting rid of them when the castle was dismantled afterwards. We are indebted to the late Sir John Cowell for the conjectural plan and description of the castle.

As soon as the Bishop had completed this much he would feel tolerably safe, but he would not be satisfied. He could hardly have room in his castle for all his retainers, and he could not command the country from it, except towards the south; therefore his next work was to make an embankment and the ditch on the outer side of it. It was then an unbroken semicircle, jutting out as it were from the castle, and protecting a sufficient space of ground for troops to encamp.

In case of an enemy forcing their way into this, the defenders could retreat into the castle by the drawbridge. The entrance was on the east side, and in order to protect this and the back of the castle, by which is meant the northern side, another embankment was made and finished with a parapet. Also as, in case of this being carried by the enemy, it would be impossible for the defenders in the northern part of the castle to run round the castle and into shelter by the main gateway, he built a square tower (exactly opposite to the ruin which yet remains), and divided from it only by the great ditch. On either side of the tower - cutting the embankment across, therefore, at right angles - was a little ditch, spanned by a drawbridge, which, if the defenders thought it necessary to retire to the tower, could at any time be raised (the foundations of the tower and the position of the ditches can still be distinctly traced). Supposing, further, that it became impossible to hold the tower, the besieged could retreat into the main body of the castle by means of another drawbridge across the great ditch, which would lead them through the arch (which can still be seen in the ruins, though it is partially blocked up). The room on the east side of this passage was probably a guard-room. In some castles of this date there were also two or three tunnels bored through the earth-work from the inner courtyard to the bottom of the great ditch, so as to provide additional ways of retreat for such men as might otherwise be cut off in those parts most distant from either of the great gates, in order to secure the outlying defence.

Henry de Blois must have been thinking of the many feudal castles of his native France. He was a magnificent prelate, though involved in the wars of his brother and the Empress Matilda. The hospital of St. Cross, and much of the beauty of Romsey Abbey, are ascribed to him, and he even endeavoured to obtain that Winchester should be raised to the dignity of a Metropolitan See. It does not appear that all his elaborate defences at Merdon were ever called into practical use; and when his brother, King Stephen, died in 1154, he fled from England, and the young Henry II. in anger dismantled Merdon, together with his other castles of Wolvesey and Waltham; nor were these fortifications ever restored. The king and bishop were reconciled; and the latter spent a pious and penitent old age, only taking one meal a day, and spending the surplus in charity. He died in 1174.

CHAPTER II - MEDIÆVAL GIFTS

It was considered in the Middle Ages that tithes might be applied to any church purpose, and were not the exclusive right of the actual parish priest, provided he obtained a sufficient maintenance, which in those days of celibacy was not very expensive. The bishops and other patrons thus assigned the great tithes of corn of many parishes to religious foundations elsewhere, only leaving the incumbent the smaller tithe from other crops - an arrangement which has resulted in many abuses.

Thus in 1301, when Bishop Sawbridge or Points, or as it was Latinised, de Pontissara, founded the college of St. Elizabeth, in St. Stephen's, Merdon, by the Itchen at Winchester, for the education of twelve poor boys by a provost and fellows, he endowed it in part with the great tithe of Hursley. The small tithes having been found insufficient for the maintenance of the vicar, he united to Hursley the rectory of Otterbourne, giving the great tithes to the vicar of Hursley; and in 1362 Bishop Edyngton confirmed the transaction.

Mr. Marsh thus relates the transaction:-

"The Living of Hursley was anciently a rectory, and, as it is believed, wholly unconnected with any other church or parish. Unfortunately, however, for the parishioners, as well as for the minister, it was, about the year 1300, reduced to a vicarage, and the great tithes appropriated to the College of St. Elizabeth in Winchester. The small tithes which remained being inadequate to the support of the vicar and his necessary assistants, the church of Otterbourne was consolidated with that of Hursley, and the tithes of that parish, both great and small, were given to them to make up a sufficient maintenance - an arrangement which, in that dark age, was thought not only justifiable but even laudable, but which nevertheless deserves to this day to be severely censured, since not only the minister but both the parishes and the cause of religion have suffered a serious and continued injury from it.

"The person by whom this appropriation was made was John de Pontissara, alias Points, Bishop of Winchester, the founder of the college to which the tithes were granted; it was, however, afterwards confirmed by William de Edyngton, by whom the vicar's rights, which before were probably undefined, and perhaps the subject of contention, were ascertained and secured to him by endowment. This instrument is still in being, bearing the date of 1362. It may be seen in Bishop Edyngton's Register, part I, fol. 128, under the following marginal title:- 'Ratificatio et Confirmatio appropriationis Ecclesiae de Hursleghe, et ordinationes Vicarie ejusd.' The following is a translation of it, so far as the vicar's interests are concerned in it:- 'The said vicar shall have and receive all and all manner of tithes, great and small, with all offerings and other emoluments belonging to the chapel of Otterbourne, situated within the parish of the said church (viz. of Hursley). He shall also have and receive all offerings belonging to the church of Hursley, and all small tithes arising within the parish of the same, viz., the tithes of cheese, milk, honey, wax, pigs, lambs, calves, eggs, chickens, geese, pigeons, flax, apples, pears, and all other tithable fruits whatsoever of curtilages or gardens. He shall also receive the tithes of mills already erected, or that shall be erected. He shall also receive and have all personal tithes of all traders, servants, labourers, and artificers whatsoever, due to the said church. The said Vicar shall also receive and have all mortuaries whatsoever, live and dead, of whatsoever things they may consist. The said Vicar shall also receive and have all profit and advantage arising from the herbage of the churchyard. He shall also have and receive the tithes of all fish-ponds whatsoever, within the said parish, wheresoever made, or that hereafter shall be made. The said Vicar shall also have for his habitation the space on the south side of the churchyard, measuring in length, from the said churchyard and the rectorial house, formerly belonging to the said church, towards the south, twenty-seven perches; and in breadth, from the hedge and ditch between the said space and the garden of the aforesaid former rectory on the west, towards the east, sixteen perches and a half, with the buildings erected thereon.'

"Besides the above, John de Pontissara allotted to the Vicar the tithes of wool, beans, and vetches; but of the first of these he was deprived by Bishop Edyngton's endowment, and the latter have been so little cultivated that he has never yet derived any advantage from them, though his right to this species of tithes cannot, I suppose, be questioned, unless, indeed, they are comprehended under the term Bladum, and are consequently to be considered as the portion of the Impropriator. The tithes given by the Endowment to the President and Chaplains of St. Elizabeth College are - 'Decimæ Bladi cujuscunque generis, Fœni ac Lanæ,' and no other.

"The church of Hursley is situated within the deanery of Winchester, and is a Peculiar; a distinction which it enjoys, probably, in consequence of its having been formerly under the patronage of the bishop. The advantages of this are, that it is not subject to the archdeacon's jurisdiction; that the minister is not obliged to attend his visitations; and that he has the privilege of granting letters of administration to wills, when the property conveyed by them lies within the limits of the vicarage.

"The value of the benefice, as rated in the King's Book, is £9 per annum, and the tenths are of course 18s. These the incumbent is required to pay annually, but he is exempted from the payment of the First Fruits. The land-tax with which the vicarage is charged is £14: 1: 2½ per annum; and the procurations and diet-money payable on account of the Bishop's Visitation amount to 12s. 9½d."

The patronage of the living, when a rectory, belonged to the bishops of Winchester, and afterwards, when reduced to a vicarage, was expressly reserved to himself and his successors by William de Edyngton; and so long as they kept possession of the Manor of Merdon, they continued patrons of the vicarage. This Bishop Edyngton, the same who began the alteration of the cathedral, is said to have built the second church of All Saints at Hurley, the tower of which still remains.

William of Wykeham, among his wider interests, seems to have had little concern with Hursley or Otterbourne.

The bishops possessed numerous manors in the diocese, and these were really not only endowments, but stations whence the episcopal duty of visitation could be performed. Riding forth with his train of clergy, chaplains, almoners, lawyers, crossbearers, and choristers, besides his household of attendants, the bishop entered a village, where the bells were rung, priest, knight, franklins, and peasants came out with all their local display, often a guild, to receive him, and other clergy gathered in; mass was said, difficulties or controversies attended to, confirmation given to the young people and children, and, after a meal, the bishop proceeded, sometimes to a noble's castle, or a convent, but more often to another manor of his own, where he was received by his resident steward or park-keeper, and took up his abode, the neighbouring clergy coming in to pay their respects, mention their grievances, and hold counsel with him. His dues were in the meantime collected, and his residence lasted as long as business, ecclesiastical or secular, required his presence, or till he and his train had eaten up the dues in kind that came in.

Whether the visit was welcome or not depended a good deal on the character of the prelate, and the hold he kept on his subordinates. The great courtly bishops, like William of Wykeham, generally sent their suffragans, titular bishops in partibus infidelium, to perform their duties.

One of the park-keepers of Merdon was judged worthy of a Latin epitaph, probably the work of a chaplain or of a Winchester scholar to whom he had endeared himself:

Hic in humo stratus, John Bowland est tumulatus

Vir pius et gratus et ab omnibus hinc peramatus

Custos parcorum praestans quondam fuit horum

De Merdon, quorum et Wintoniæ dominorum.

Hic quinqgenis hinc octenis rite deemptis

   Cum plausu gentis custos erat in eis.

Festum Clementis tempus fuerat morientis

Mille quadringentis annis Christi redimentis,

Quadris his junctis simul et cum septuagintis.

   Hunc cum defunctis, protege, Christe, tuis.

Here laid in the ground, John Bowland hath sepulture,

A man of faith and kindliness, and hence by all beloved.

He was aforetime the excellent guardian of this park

Belonging to certain lords of Merdon and Winchester.

He for (lit. in) 50 years - (8 being taken away precisely)

   With the applause of all the community was guardian among them.

The Festival of Clement was his date of dying

In years one thousand four hundred after Christ's Redemption,

Adding to these four (?) (years) and seventy.

   Him, O Christ, befriend with those who are thine!

Unlike Hursley, or rather the Manor of Merdon, Otterbourne had many different possessors in succession, and is even at the present day divided into various holdings on different tenures.

In 1244 Walter and John de Brompton, sons of Sir Bryan de Brompton, lived at Hayswode, a name now lost or changed into "Otterbourne Park," the wood spreading over the east side of the hill. At the same time Sir Henry de Capella was possessor of the manor; but in 1265 it had passed, by what means we do not know, to Sir Francis de Bohun - a very early specimen of this Christian name which was derived from the sobriquet of the Saint of Assisi, whose Christian name was John.

From the son of Sir Francis in 1279 Simon the Draper obtained the Manor of Otterbourne for 600 merks, and a quit rent of a pair of gilt spurs valued at six pence! Simon seems to have assumed the gilt spurs himself, for he next appears as "Sir Simon de Wynton." Indeed it seems that knighthood might be conferred on the possessors of a certain amount of land. Wynton in two more generations has lengthened into Wynchester, when, in 1379, the manor is leased to Hugh Croans, merchant, and Isabella his wife for their lives, paying after the first twenty-five years £100 per annum. And two years later William de Winchester conveyed the manor over to Hugh Croans or Crans.

The great Bishop William of Wykeham bought it in 1386, and gave it to his cousin, bearing the same name. It continued in the Wykeham family till 1458, when William Fiennes or Fenys, Lord Say and Sele, the son of him who was murdered by Jack Cade's mob, being married to the heiress, Margaret Wykeham, sold it to Bishop Waynflete for £600.

The bishop's treasurer was Hugh Pakenham; and being one of the feoffees to whom the manor was conveyed for the bishop, he pretended that he had bought it for himself, and absconded with some of the title deeds; but eventually he died in magna miseria in sanctuary at St. Martin's le Grand, Westminster. His son John renounced the pretended claim, and very generously the Bishop gave him £40.

In 1481, good Bishop Waynflete made over the property to his newly-founded College of St. Mary Magdalen at Oxford, in whose possession it has remained ever since, except small portions which have been enfranchised from time to time. It includes Otterbourne hill, with common land on the top and wood upon the slope, as well as various meadows and plough lands. The manor house, still bearing the name of the Moat House, was near the old church in the meadows, and entirely surrounded with its own moat. It must have been a house of some pretension in the sixteenth century, for there is a handsome double staircase, a rough fresco in one room, and in the lowest there was a panel over the fireplace, with a painting representing apparently a battle between Turks and Austrians. The President of Magdalen College on progress always held his court there. The venerable Dr. Rowth in extreme old age was the last who did so. Since his time the bridge crossing the moat fell in and choked it; it became a marsh; the farm was united to another, the picture removed, and the only inhabitants are such a labourer's family as may be impervious to the idea that it is haunted.

Simon the Draper, otherwise Sir Simon de Wynton, granted a plot of land to the north-west of the Manor House to Adam de Lecke in villeinage, and later in freehold to John de Otterbourne, reserving thirteen shillings rent. By this last it was rented on his wife Alice, from whom it passed through several hands to John Colpoys in the year of Henry VI., and twenty-two years later this same John Colpoys agreed with the warden and fellows of Winchester College to enfeoff them of one messuage, four tofts, twenty acres of arable land, and eighteen acres of meadow, to the intent that they should on the 7th day of April in every year celebrate the obits of Alice his deceased wife, of John Giles and Maud his wife (her parents), of Sir John Shirborne and of Joan Parke, and of Colpoys himself and Joan his then wife, after their respective deaths.

These obits, namely anniversaries of deaths when masses were to be offered for the person recollected, were to be secured by the fee of a shilling to the warden on each occasion, sixpence to each fellow and chaplain, and likewise to the schoolmaster, twopence to each lay clerk, sixpence to the sacrist for wax candles, and a mark or thirteen and fourpence to be spent in a "pittance" extra course in the college hall. The indenture by which Colpoys hoped to secure perpetual masses in remembrance of his relations and himself is in perfect preservation, with seals attached, in the muniment chamber of Winchester College.

The property has continued ever since in the possession of the College of St. Mary, Winchester, though the masses ceased to be celebrated after the Reformation.

In those days the rector of Hursley was John de Ralegh, probably a kinsman of the bishop of that name.

Before this, however, Bishop Richard Toclive had a dispute with the Knights of St. John, who claimed the almshouse of Noble Poverty at St. Cross as Hospitallers. They had unfortunately a reputation for avarice, and Toclive bought them off by giving them the impropriation of Merton and Hursleigh for 53 marks a year.

PAGANUS DE LYSKERET, styled Presbyter, was collated in 1280. It appears that at this time there was a perpetual vicar established in the Church of Hursley as well as a rector; and that he was instituted by the bishop, had a certain fixed maintenance assigned to him, and was independent of the rector. In the register of John de Pontissera, Bishop of Winton, may now be seen what is there called the "Ordinatio Episcopi inter Rectorem et Vicarium de Hurslegh." It is therein settled that the vicar shall have a house as described and other emoluments, and that the rector shall pay to him forty shillings per annum. The vicar at this time was Johannes de Sta. Fide. The deed of settlement was executed in Hyde Abbey, in the year 1291; Philip de Barton, John de Ffleming, William de Wenling, and others being witnesses to it. Vide Regist. de Pontissera, fol. 10. Forty shillings or five marks was, it appears, the stipend usually assigned to vicars and curates at this time, the vicar being really what we now call a curate.

HUGO DE WELEWYCK, styled Clericus, succeeded in 1296 on the resignation of Paganus and was the last rector, the benefice having in his time been reduced to a vicarage by the appropriation of the rectorial-house, tithes, and glebe to the College of St. Elizabeth. The pretences assigned for this act, for true reasons they could scarcely be, since in all cases of appropriation and consolidation they appear to have been almost exactly the same, were the unfinished state of the college buildings and the insufficiency of the revenues for the maintenance of the society, owing to wars, sickness, pestilence, and the like. But notwithstanding this serious deprivation and loss, a vicar it appears was still continued in the church, Hugh de Welewyck having presented two, viz. Henricus de Lyskeret in 1300, and Roger de la Vere in 1302; of whom the latter was certainly appointed after the appropriation.

WILLIAM DE FFARLEE was collated Vicar of Hursley, on the death of Welewyck in 1348.

WILLIAM DE MIDDLETON was collated in 1363.

CHAPTER III - REFORMATION TIMES

The rectorial tithe of Hursley having been given to St. Elizabeth's College, and apparently some rights over Merdon, the Chancellor Wriothesley obtained that, on the confiscation of monastic property, the manor should be granted to him. Stephen Gardiner had been bishop since 1531, a man who, though he had consented to the king's assumption of the royal supremacy, grieved over the fact as an error all his life. He appeared at the bar of the House of Commons and pleaded the rights of his See, to which Merdon had belonged for 1300 years. It was probably in consequence of his pleading that Wriothesley restored the manor, but when Gardiner was illegally deposed by the regency of Edward VI. on 14th February 1550, John Poynet, a considerable scholar, but a man of disgraceful life, obtained the appointment to the see, by alienating various estates to the Seymour family, and Merdon was resumed by the Crown. It was then granted to Sir Philip Hobby who had been one of King Henry's privy councillors, and had been sent on an embassy to Portugal, attended by ten gentlemen of his own retinue, wearing velvet coats with chains of gold.

Already had come to the hamlet of Slackstead in Hursley Parish another reformer, Thomas Sternhold, who had been gentleman of the bed-chamber to Henry VIII., and had put thirty-seven Psalms into English verse, in hopes of improving the morals of the Court. John Hopkins and Robert Wisdom completed the translation of the Psalms, which Fuller in his history says was at first derided and scoffed at as piety rather than poetry, adding that the good gentleman had drunk more of Jordan than of Helicon. In his Worthies, however, he says: "He was afterwards (saith my author) ab intimo cubiculo to

King Edward the Sixth; though I am not satisfied whether thereby he meant gentleman of his privy chamber or groom of his bed-chamber. He was a principal instrument of translating the Psalms into English metre; the first twenty-six (and seven-and-thirty in all) being by him performed. Yet had he other assistance in that work. Many a bitter scoff hath since been passed on their endeavours by some wits, which might have been better employed. Some have miscalled these their translations Geneva gigs (i.e. jigs); and which is the worst, father (or mother rather) the expression on our virgin queen, as falsely as other things have been charged upon her. Some have not sticked to say 'that David hath been as much persecuted by bungling translators as by Saul himself.' Some have made libellous verses in abuse of them, and no wonder if songs were made on the translators of the Psalms, seeing drunkards made them on David the author thereof.

"But let these translations be beheld by impartial eyes, and they will be allowed to go in equipage with the best poems in that age. However, it were to be wished that some bald rhymes therein were bettered; till which time, such as sing them must endeavour to amend them by singing them with understanding heads and gracious hearts, whereby that which is bad metre on earth will be made good music in heaven. As for our Thomas Sternhold, it was happy for him that he died before his good master, anno 1549, in the month of August; so probably preventing much persecution which had happened unto him if surviving in the reign of Queen Mary."

Such was Fuller's judgment and that of the author he quotes, nevertheless the version of the Psalms, being printed with the Prayer-Book, took such a strong hold of the nation that in 1798 Hannah More was accused of dissent, because the version of Tate and Brady was used in her schools. Mr. Keble preferred it to this latter as more like the Hebrew, and some of his versions (curiously enough proceeding from the same parish) remind us of these simple old translators. The Old Hundredth, and in some degree the 23rd and the opening of the 18th, still hold their place, probably in virtue of the music to which they are wedded.

Bishop Gardiner recovered the Manor of Merdon, with his liberty, on Queen Mary's accession. Then it was that Philip of Spain rode through one of these villages, probably Otterbourne, soaked through with rain, on his way to his ill-starred marriage with Mary.

Gardiner was no persecutor, and Sternhold's widow lived on at Slackstede. On his death, Queen Mary gave the diocese to John White, the same who preached to Elizabeth on a living dog being better than a dead lion.

Hobby then claimed the manor, but Bishop White made a strenuous resistance, appealing to Gardiner's former plea, and supported by the Attorney General Story, who is said to have been an enemy of Sir Philip Hobby. The case was argued in the House of Lords, and given against the bishop, though under the protest of several of the Lords Spiritual, who dreaded the like treatment.

Story was prosecuted by the Commons for pleading before the Lords, fled to the Netherlands and was trepanned on board an English ship, and put to death as a traitor.

Bishop White was deprived the next year, and retired to his sister's house at South Warnborough, where he died. Queen Elizabeth is said to have visited him.

Merdon was thus in 1558 for ever alienated from the diocese of Winchester. Sir Philip Hobby is said to have first built the Lodge, as it was called, of Hursley Park, about a quarter of a mile from Merdon Castle, which had become ruinous. Those were the days when the massive walls and minute comfortless chambers were deserted, defence being less thought of than convenience in our happy country; and indeed Sir Philip seems to have used Hursley as a residence instead of only a shelter on a tour. He died at Bisham aged 53, on the 31st of May 1558, soon after his victory over the See of Winchester, and is there buried, as well as his elder brother, Sir Thomas. He left no children, and was succeeded by his brother William, who had married the widow of Sternhold. On her death the following memorial was erected over a stone bearing the coat, "On a chevron embattled, between three griffins' heads erased, three roses; and on a brass the inscription:

If ever chaste or honest godly lyfe

Myght merit prayse . of everlastyng fame

Forget not then . that worthy Sternhold's wife

Our Hobbie's make . Anne Horswell cald by name

From whome alas . to sone for hers here left

Hath God her Soule . deth her lyfe byreft,

Anno 1559."

His property at Hursley descended to his son Giles Hobby, Esq., who, it appears clearly by the register and other records, was living in the parish very early in the seventeenth century. His last wife was Ann, the daughter of Sir Thomas Clarke, Knight of Avyngton in Berkshire, to whom he sold the castle and manor of Merdon, reserving, however to himself and wife, a life-holding in the lodge and park. When this sale was made does not appear, but it is supposed to have been before the year 1602, as Sir Thomas was then living at Merdon, and his son married in that year at Hursley. Giles Hobby died in the year 1626, and his wife in 1630. They were both buried at Hursley, probably in the church, but no monument appears to have been erected to their memory.

"Sir Thomas Clarke may be considered as the next lord of Merdon, though he was never in possession of either the lodge or the park, and held only for a few years what he did possess. So long, however, as he continued proprietor of the manor, it is said that he lived at Merdon, I suppose at the castle, a part of which was probably then standing and habitable. Sir Thomas, it would seem, kept the demesne lands in his own occupation, requiring the tenants or copyholders of the manor, according to ancient usage, to perform the customary service of reaping and housing his crops: (1) The days employed in this service were called Haydobyn days; (2) and during their continuance the lord was obliged to provide breakfast and dinner for the workmen. Richard Morley, in his Manuscript, gives a very curious account of a quarrel which occurred on one of these occasions. 'Another time' (says he) 'upon a haydobyn-day (320 or 340 reapers) the cart brought a-field for them a hogshead of porridge, which stunk and had worms swimming in it. The reapers refused to work without better provisions. Mr. Coram of Cranbury would not suffer them to work. Mr. Pye, Sir Thomas Clarke's steward, and Coram drew their daggers, and rode at each other through the wheat. At last Lady Clarke promised to dress for them two or three hogs of bacon: twenty nobles' work lost.' He adds, that 'a heire (hire) went for a man on the haydobyn-days, if able to carry a hooke a-field.'"

This "haydobyn" is supposed by Mr. Marsh to be a corruption of the old word "haydogtime," a word signifying a country dance. It seems that when the tenants were called on to perform work in hedging, reaping, or hay-making, upon the lands of the lord of the manor, in lieu of money rent he was bound to feed them through the day, and generally to conclude with a merry-making. So, no doubt, it had been in the good old days of the bishops and the much loved and lamented John Bowland; but harder times had come with Sir Thomas Clarke, when it required the interference of Mr. Coram of Cranbury to secure them even an eatable meal. No doubt such stout English resistance saved the days of compulsory labour from becoming a burden intolerable as in France.

Roger Coram, gent., rented Cranbury at £17: 2s. Cranbury is a low wooded hill, then part of the manor of Merdon, nearly two miles to the south-east of Hursley, and in that parish, though nearer to Otterbourne. Several tenements seem to have been there, those in the valley being called Long Moor and Pot Kiln. Shoveller is the first name connected with Cranbury, but Mr. Roger Coram, the champion of the haymakers, held it till his death, when it passed to Sir Edward Richards.

On the other hand, Brambridge, which stands in Twyford parish, but held part of the hundred of Boyatt in Otterbourne, was in the hands of the Roman Catholic family of Welles, who seem to have had numerous retainers at

Highbridge, Allbrook, and Boyatt. Swithun Welles made Brambridge a refuge for priests, and two or three masses were said in his house each day. One "Ben Beard," a spy, writes in 1584 that if certain priests were not at Brambridge they would probably be at Mr. Strange's at Mapledurham, where was a hollow place by the livery cupboard capable of containing two men.

Swithun Welles went later to London and took a house in Holborn, where Topcliffe the priest-catcher broke in on Father Genings saying mass, and both he and Mr. Welles were hanged together for what was adjudged in those days to be a treasonable offence, implying disaffection to the Queen.

The modern house of Brambridge affords no priests' chambers. It is believed that an older one was burnt down, and there is a very dim report that a priest was drowned in a stone basin in a neighbouring wood.

The register of Twyford Church contains the record of a number of the Welles family buried in the churchyard clandestinely, by night. John Wells, mentioned in the Athenæ Oxoniensis as an able man living at Deptford, retired to Brambridge, and died there in 1634. This accounts for there having been the Roman Catholic school at Twyford, whence Alexander Pope was expelled for some satirical verses on the master. The house is still known.

The vicars of Hursley at this period were John Hynton, presented by Bishop Gardiner, but deprived in on account of his tenets. Richard Fox was presented in his place by William Hobby. It must have been owing to the reforming zeal of this vicar of Hursley that the frescoes in Otterbourne Church were as far as possible effaced, white-washed over, and the Ten Commandments painted over them in old English lettering, part of which was still legible in 1839. Otterbourne was apparently still served by the vicar of Hursley or his assistant.

Parish Registers began at this date, and here are the remarkable occurrences recorded at Hursley:

EXTRAORDINARY OCCURRENCES, ETC.

1582. A great hail storm happened at Hursley, Baddesley, and in the neighbourhood, this year. The hail-stones measured nine inches in circumference.

1604. The plague made its appearance at Anfield. It broke out in November, and continued till the following February. Many persons died of it, and were not brought to the church, but buried in the waste near their residence.

1610. A person of the name of Wooll hanged himself at Gosport, in the parish of Hursley, about this time. He was buried at the corner of Newland's Coppice, and a stake was driven through his body. (The place still bears the name of Newland's Coppice.)

1621. A planked thrashing-floor first laid down in the parish this year, viz. at

Merdon. Chalk-floors used before. It was reckoned a memorable improvement.

1629. A great fall of snow in October. It was nearly half a foot deep, and remained on the ground three or four days.

1635. A copyholder was hanged for murder this year. His copyhold was seized by the lord as forfeited, but afterwards recovered, viz. in 1664.

CHAPTER IV - PURITAN TIMES

After his dispute with the haymakers, Sir Thomas Clarke sold Merdon to William Brock, a lawyer, from whom it passed to John Arundel, and then to Sir Nathanael Napier, whose son, Sir Gerald, parted with it again to Richard Maijor, the son of the mayor of Southampton. This was in 1638, and for some time the lodge at Hursley was lent to Mr. Kingswell, Mr. Maijor's father-in-law, who died there in 1639, after which time Mr. Maijor took up his abode there. He seems to have been a shrewd, active man, and a staunch Protestant, for when there was a desire to lease out Cranbury, he, as Lord of the Manor, stipulated that it should be let only to a Protestant of the Church of England, not to a Papist. The neighbourhood of the Welleses at Brambridge probably moved him to make this condition.

The person who applied for the lease was Dr. John Young, Dean of Winchester, who purchased the copyhold of Cranbury before 1643, and retired thither when he was expelled from his deanery and other preferments in the evil times of the Commonwealth, and there died, leaving his widow in possession.

Whether the lady was molested by Mr. Maijor we do not know. He was no favourite with Richard Morley, who rented the forge in Hursley, the farm of Ratlake and Anvyle, as Ampfield was then spelt, and thought him a severe lord to his copyholders. Morley was born at Hursley, and was sent to school at Baddesley in 1582, the year of the great hailstorm of the nine-inch stones. He kept valuable memoranda, which Mr. Marsh quotes, and died in 1672, when he is registered as:-

"Ricardus Morley Senex sepultus fuit, August 1672." (Senex indeed, for he must have been 97.)

Of Maijor, Morley records, "He was very witty and thrifty, and got more by oppressing his tenants than did all the lords in 60 years before him. He was a justice of the peace, and raised a troop in the cause of the Parliament." It must have been in the army that Oliver Cromwell made his acquaintance, and in 1647 began the first proposals of a "Marriage treaty," between Richard,

Oliver's eldest surviving son, just twenty-one and educated for the Law, and the elder daughter of Mr. Maijor (which Carlyle always spells as Mayor). For the time, however, this passed off; but, apparently under the direction of Mr. Robertson, a minister of Southampton, and Mr. Stapylton, also a minister, the treaty was resumed; and three weeks after the King's execution, Oliver wrote to Mr. Maijor.

For my very worthy friend, Richard Mayor, Esq.: These.

LONDON, 12th February 1648.

SIR - I received some intimations formerly, and by the last return from Southampton a Letter from Mr. Robinson, concerning the reviving of the last year's motion, touching my Son and your Daughter. Mr. Robinson was also pleased to send enclosed in his, a Letter from you, bearing date the 5th of this instant, February, wherein I find your willingness to entertain any good means for the completing of that business.

From whence I take encouragement to send my Son to wait upon you; and by him to let you know, that my desires are, if Providence so dispose, very full and free to the thing, - if upon an interview, there prove also a freedom in the young persons thereunto. What liberty you will give herein, I wholly submit to you. I thought fit, in my Letter to Mr. Robinson, to mention somewhat of expedition because indeed I know not how soon I may be called into the field, or other occasions may remove me from hence; having for the present some liberty of stay in London. The Lord direct all to His glory. - I rest, Sir, your very humble servant,

OLIVER CROMWELL.

Probably this was the time when the public-house of Hursley took the name of "The King's Head," which it has kept to the present day. But young Cromwell was inclined to loyalty, and when at Cambridge used to drink "to the health of our landlord," meaning the King! He was one-and-twenty when, with his father's friend Mr. Stapylton, he made a visit to Hursley, and was received by Mr. and Mrs. Maijor with many civilities, also seeing their two daughters, Dorothy and Anne. In a letter of 28th February, Cromwell thanks Mr. Maijor for "The reception of my son, in the liberty given him to wait on your worthy daughter, the report of whose virtues and godliness has so great a place in my heart that I think fit not to neglect anything on my part which may consummate a close of the business, if God please to dispose the young ones' hearts thereunto, and other suitable ordering of affairs towards mutual satisfaction appear in the dispensation of Providence."

Mr. Stapylton was commissioned to act for General Cromwell in the matter of settlements, over which there was considerable haggling, though Oliver writes that "the report of the young lady's godliness causeth him to deny himself in the matter of moneys." More correspondence ensued, as to the settlement of Hursley upon Dorothy and her heirs male, and the compensation to her younger sister Anne. Cromwell was anxious to hurry on the matter so as to have it concluded before his departure to take the command in Ireland.

The terms were finally settled, and Richard and Dorothy were married at Hursley on May Day, 1649, before Cromwell's departure to crush the ill-arranged risings in Ireland. Her sister Anne shortly after married John Dunch of Baddesley, with £1000 as her portion. Morley of Baddesley chronicles the marriage in no friendly tone: "When" (says he) "King Charles was put to death, and Oliver Cromwell Protector of England, and Richard Maijor of his privy council, and Noll his eldest son Richard married to Mr. Maijor's daughter Doll, then Mr. Maijor did usurp authority over his tenants at Hursley." In another place he says that "he" (i.e. Mr. Maijor) "set forth horse and man for the Parliament, and was a captain and justice of peace. Lord Richard Cromwell was also a justice of peace, and John Dunch a captain and justice. These all lived at Lodge together in Oliver's reign; so we had justice right or wrong by power; for if we did offend, they had power to send us a thousand miles off, and that they have told us."

Richard, having no turn for politics or warfare, preferred to live a quiet life with his father-in-law, in the lodge. There were two walnut avenues planted about this time, leading to the lodge from the churchyard on one side, and on the other towards Baddesley; and the foundations of the house can still be traced on the lawn to which both lead.

Oliver writes in the summer after the marriage that he is glad the young people have leisure to make a journey to eat cherries. There is little doubt but that this must have been to the gardens in Ram-Alley near Chandler's Ford, originally Chaloner's Ford, where numerous trees, bearing quantities of little black cherries called merries, used to grow, and where parties used to go as a Sunday diversion, and eat, before the days of the station and the building.

The elder Mrs. Cromwell paid a visit to Hursley after parting with the Protector on his voyage to Ireland; but he never seems to have gone thither in person, though he wrote kindly paternal letters to his son and daughter. He wishes Richard to study mathematics and cosmography, and read history, especially Sir Walter Raleigh's. "It is a Body of history, and will add much more to your understanding than fragments of story." And to Dorothy, he gives advice on her health and religious habits.

John Hardy had been Vicar of Hursley but was expelled, and Mr. Maijor, as patron of the living, provided persons for the ministry and kept a close account of their expenses, which is still preserved. Seven different ministers in the half year after Christmas 1645 were remunerated "for travell and pains in preaching," after which time Mr. Richard Webb settled for a time at Hursley, and Mr. Daniel Lloyd at Otterbourne, though several more changes took place.

A parish register at Hursley, 1653, recording births (not baptisms), mentions the opening of a chalk-pit at Hatchgate in 1655, and at Otterbourne. The children of William Downe of Otterbourne Farm are distinguished by double black lines below their names.

Oliver Cromwell, according to an old village tradition, sunk his treasure at the bottom of Merdon Well, in an iron chest which must have been enchanted, for, on an endeavour to draw it up, no one was to speak. One workman unfortunately said, "Here it comes," when it immediately sank to the bottom and (this is quite certain) never was seen! The well was cleaned out in later times, and nothing was found but a pair of curious pattens, cut away to receive a high-heeled shoe, also a mazer-bowl, an iron flesh-hook and small cooking-pot, and a multitude of pins, thrown in to make the curious reverberating sound when, after several seconds, they reached the water. A couple of ducks are said to have been thrown down, and to have emerged at Pool hole at Otterbourne with their feathers scraped off.

On 3rd September 1658, the family party at Hursley was broken up by the unexpected death of the Protector. He was not yet sixty years of age, and had not contemplated being cut off before affairs were more settled; and when, in his last moments, he was harassed with enquiries as to his successor, he answered, "You will find my will in such a drawer of my cabinet." Some of his counsellors thought he named his son Richard; and no one ever found the drawer with the will in it, in which it was thought that his son-in-law Fleetwood, a much abler man, was named.

At any rate, Richard was accepted in his father's place by Parliament and army, and went to much expense for the Protector's funeral. It must have been a great misfortune to him that his shrewd father-in-law, the witty and thrifty Mr. Maijor, was sinking under a complication of incurable diseases, of which Morley speaks somewhat unkindly, and he died in the end of April 1660.

Richard had never been a strong partisan of the Commonwealth, though he had quietly submitted to whatever was required of him. He had been member of Parliament for the county of Hants, and had been placed at the head of the list of his father's attempt at a House of Lords, and he allowed greatness to be thrust on him in a quiet acquiescent way. He dismissed the fictitious parliament that his father had summoned, and then offended the strict and godly of the army by promoting soldiers of whom they disapproved. "Here is Dick Ingoldsby," he said; "he can neither pray nor preach, and yet I trust him before you all."

No one had any real enthusiasm for the harmless, helpless man, "the phantom king of half a year"; and it was just as old Mr. Maijor was dying that Richard was requested by the "Rump" to resign, and return to Hampton Court, with the promise of a pension and of payment of the debts incurred by his father. While packing for his departure, he sat down on a box containing all the complimentary addresses made to him, and said, "Between my legs lie the lives and fortunes of all the good folk in England!" He then returned to Hursley, where he found himself pursued by those debts of his father which the Long Parliament had engaged to pay, and which swallowed up more than his patrimony, though the manor of Merdon, having been settled upon his wife, could not be touched. He was sufficiently alarmed, however, to make him retreat to the continent and change his name to Clarke.

In 1675 Mrs. Richard Cromwell died, leaving out of a numerous family only one son and two daughters. The son, Oliver, inherited the estates, and seems to have been on good terms with his father, who, in 1700, came to live at Cheshunt under his name of Clarke, and made some visits to Hursley. Richard married under this assumed name, and left some children.

When Oliver died without heirs in 1706, his father Richard, according to the original settlement, succeeded to the property, but his two daughters set up their claim, and the case was brought into court. It is said that the judge was Cowper, but this has been denied. At any rate the judge seems to have been shocked at the undutiful litigation, and treated the old man with much respect.

The case was decided in his favour, and he lived between Hursley and Cheshunt till his death in 1712 in his 86th year.

As Mr. Palgrave writes:-

Him count we wise,

Him also, though the chorus of the throng

Be silent, though no pillar rise

In slavish adulation of the strong,

But here, from blame of tongues and fame aloof,

'Neath a low chancel roof,

The peace of God

He sleeps; unconscious hero! Lowly grave

By village footsteps daily trod;

Unconscious! or while silence holds the nave,

And the bold robin comes, when day is dim,

And pipes his heedless hymn.

These are a poet's meditations on him, more graceful than the inscription on the monument erected to him by his two undutiful daughters, ere, in 1718, they sold the estate. It was a large tablet of marble, surmounted by death's heads. It is of gray or veined marble, in the Doric style of architecture, and is in height thirteen feet, and in breadth nearly nine. The inscription upon it is as follows:-

This Monument was erected to the memory of Mrs. Eliz. Cromwell, spinster (by Mr. Richard Cromwell and Thomas Cromwell, her executors). She died the 8th day of April 1731, in the 82d yeare of her age, and lyes interred near this place; she was the daughter of Richard Cromwell, Esq., by Dorothy, his wife, who was the daughter of Richard Maijor, Esq. And the following account of her family (all of whom, except Mrs. Ann Gibson, lie in this chancel) is given according to her desire.

Mrs. Ann Gibson, the 6th daughter, died 7th Dec. 1727, in the 69th year of her age, and lies interred, with Dr. Thomas Gibson, her husband, Physician General of the Army, in the church-yard belonging to St. George's Chapel, in London.

Richard Cromwell, Esq., father of the said Eliz. Cromwell, died 12th July 1712, in the 86th year of his age.

Oliver Cromwell, Esq., son of the said Richard Cromwell, died 11th May 1705, in the 49th year of his age.

Mrs. Dorothy Mortimer, a seventh daughter, wife of John Mortimer, Esq., died 14th May 1681, in the 21st year of her age, but left no issue.

Mrs. Dorothy Cromwell, wife of the said Richard Cromwell, died 5th January 1675, in the 49th year of her age.

Mrs. Ann Maijor, mother of the said Mrs. Dorothy Cromwell, died 13th of June 1662.

Richard Maijor, Esq., husband of the said Mrs. Ann Maijor, died 25th April 1660.

Mrs. Dorothy Cromwell, a fifth daughter, died 13th December 1658, in the 2nd year of her age.

A fourth daughter died 27th May 1655, in the 1st year of her age.

Mrs. Mary Cromwell, a third daughter, died 24th September 1654, in the 2nd year of her age.

A son of the said Richard and Dorothy Cromwell, died 13th December 1652, in the 1st year of his age.

Mrs. Ann Cromwell, a second daughter, died 14th March 1651, in the 1st year of her age.

Mr. John Kingswell, father of the said Mrs. Ann Maijor, died 5th March 1639.

The lime-trees, beautifully surrounding the churchyard, are said to have been planted by Richard Cromwell, and there was certainly an excellent fashion of planting them in the latter end of the seventeenth century, partly due to a French custom, partly to Evelyn's Sylva. The beautiful avenue of limes at Brambridge, in three aisles, was probably planted at this date by one of the Welles family.

In taking down the old lodge of Merdon or Hursley, a large lump of metal was found, squeezed into a crevice of the wall, and was sold by Mr. Heathcote as a Roman weight; but on being cleaned, it proved to be the die of the seal of the Commonwealth. Richard had caused a new seal to be made for himself by Simon, a noted medallist, and he had probably thus disposed of the die as a dangerous possession. Mr. Vertue saw it in 1710, in the collection of a Mr. Roberts, but it has since disappeared.

There was a stone inscribed to Edward Reynell and Mary his wife, who died respectively in 1698 and 1699. They are believed to have been friends of Oliver Cromwell the grandson, who certainly named them in his will. There was a tradition in Hursley that this Reynell was actually the executioner of King Charles.

CHAPTER V - CUSTOMS OF THE MANOR OF MERDON

As it was just at this time that the customs of the manor of Merdon were revised, this seems to be the fittest place for giving Mr. Marsh's summary of them.

"The quantity of land in cultivation within the Manor of Merdon or parish of Hursley is, as I imagine, not less than three-fifths of the whole, or about 6000 acres; of which the greater part was anciently copyhold, under the Bishop and Church of Winchester. The tenure by which it was held, was, and indeed is still, that denominatedBorough English, the most singular custom of which is, that the youngest son inherits the copyhold of his father, in preference of all his elder brothers. The origin of this tenure, according to Sir William Blackstone, is very remote, it being his opinion that it was 'a remnant of Saxon liberty'; and was so named in contradistinction to the Norman customs, afterwards introduced by the Conqueror, from the Duchy of Normandy. The reasons commonly assigned for the peculiar usage just mentioned are given by Blackstone, but they are evidently not satisfactory to him, and, as it should seem, not founded on truth. His own way of accounting for it is far more rational and probable, though, it must be confessed, it is only conjectural. He supposes that the ancient inhabitants of this island were for the most part herdsmen and shepherds; that their elder sons, as soon as they arrived at manhood, received from their father a certain allotment of cattle, and removed from him, and that the youngest son, who continued to the last with him, became naturally the heir of the family and of the remaining property.

Whether this were really the case or not will probably ever remain a question of great uncertainty; and it is a circumstance of too trifling a nature to deserve much investigation. It is, however, worthy of remark that to this day this custom of descent to the youngest son prevails among the Tartars; and that something very like it was anciently the usage among most northern nations. But whatever be its origin, or in whatever way it be accounted for, such is the custom now existing in this manor; and I have had frequent opportunities of observing that it is held, especially by the inferior class of copyholders, as sacred, and that they would, on no consideration, divert their tenements out of the customary order of inheritance.

"But besides this custom, there are others also in this manor which indicate great antiquity, and which, there can be but little if any doubt, are the same as were in use before the Norman Conquest. We are told, indeed, by Judge Blackstone, that after that event the ancient Saxon system of tenure was laid aside, and that the Normans, wherever they had lands granted to them, introduced the feodal system; and that at length it was adopted generally, and as constitutional, throughout the kingdom. There does not, however, I think, appear to be sufficient reason for supposing that this new system was received into this manor, the customs here in use being evidently those of a more remote age, and in their circumstances, if not in their nature, altogether unlike those which were at this time established by the Normans.

"Under the feodal system, the tenant originally held his lands entirely at the will of the lord, and at his death they reverted to the lord again. The services to be performed for the lord were uncertain and unlimited. The copyhold was also subject to a variety of grievous taxes, which the lord had the privilege, upon many occasions, of imposing - such as aids, reliefs, primer seisin, wardship, escheats for felony and want of heirs, and many more, altogether so exorbitant and oppressive as often totally to ruin the tenant and rob him of almost all interest in his property. The difference of the circumstances under which the lands in the manor of Merdon are, and, as it seems, always were held, is remarkably striking: here the copyhold is hereditary, the services are certain and limited, the fines are fixed and unchangeable, the lord has no right of wardship, neither is the copyhold liable to escheat for felony; the widow of a tenant has also a right of inheritance, and the tenement may be let without the lord's consent for a year. All which circumstances appear to bespeak an original and fundamental difference of tenure from that of the feodal system, and are, I presume, to be considered, not as encroachments that have gradually grown upon that system, but as being of a more liberal extraction and much greater antiquity. {57a But besides these differences, the supposition here advanced has this farther ground to rest upon, viz. that neither the name of Merdon, nor that of Hursley, is so much as mentioned in the great survey of the kingdom, called Domesday-Book, which, if the intention of that survey be rightly understood, {57b it seems next to a certainty that one or other of them would have been had the new system been here adopted. Nor, when it is considered that this was Church property, and that in many instances the alterations were not enforced, out of favour as it is supposed to the landholder, who was partial to the more ancient tenure, ought it to be thought extraordinary that the customs in this manor did not undergo the general change; since, if favour were desirable and shown to any, who were so likely to expect and to find it as the clergy? But however this point may really be, it appears evident that the tenants of this manor have, from the earliest times to which we have the means of resorting for information, enjoyed many unusual rights and immunities, and that their services were, in many respects, far from being so base and servile as those of the strictly feudal tenant.

"When it was that disputes first arose between the lord and tenants concerning their respective rights is not, I believe, known with certainty; but it appears that in the time of Mr. Maijor many of the lord's claims were complained of by the tenants as usurpations; as, on the other hand, many of theirs were by the lord as new and uncustomary. But it was in vain then for the tenants either to resist the lord's pretensions or to assert their own; such being Mr. Maijor's power and interest with the Cromwellian Government as to enable him, as they well knew, easily to defeat all their efforts. In justice, however, to Mr. Maijor, it should be mentioned that he acted, in one instance at least, with great liberality towards the tenants; as by him it was that the customary personal services were commuted for pecuniary payments - an exchange which could not fail of being peculiarly acceptable to them, as they were not only relieved by it from a service they considered as a grievance, and performed reluctantly, but had the prospect of being in the end great gainers by it. But though by this concession on the part of the lord some ground of discontent was removed, yet disputes and animosities still continued to subsist with respect to other customs; and no sooner was Mr. Maijor dead, and the Cromwell family dispossessed of its power, than the tenants laid aside their fears and renewed their opposition. The circumstances of the times being now in their favour, it might perhaps have been expected that they, in their turn, should establish all their claims without contention. The case, however, was quite otherwise, as neither Mrs. Cromwell nor her son would tamely forego any one of their supposed privileges - on the contrary, Oliver defended them in the true spirit of a Cromwell, and relinquished none but such as the decisions of a jury, which were more than once resorted to, deprived him of. In this state of strife and litigation things continued until the year 1692, when most of the principal tenants concurred in a determination to appeal to the Court of Chancery. A bill of complaint was accordingly presented to the Court, stating their supposed grievances, and soliciting its interference. Several hearings and trials, ordered in consequence of this application, for the investigation of the disputed customs, then ensued; after which, though not till more than six years had elapsed, the Court finally adjudged and decreed the customs of the manor to be, and continue for the future, as they here follow:-

"Custom 1. That all the copyholds and customary messuages, lands, and tenements within the said manor are, and have been time out of mind, copyholds of inheritance, demised and demisable to the copyholders or customary tenants thereof, and their heirs in fee simple by copy of Court Roll, according to the custom of the said manor.

"Custom 2. That the customary tenements within the said manor do descend, and ought to descend, as tenements of the tenure, and in the nature of Borough-English, not only to the youngest son or youngest daughter, and for default of such issue of such customary tenant to the youngest brother or youngest sister, but also, for default of such brother and sister of such customary tenant, to the next kinsman or kinswoman of the whole blood of the customary tenant in possession, how far so ever remote.

"Custom 3. That if any tenant of any copyhold die, seized of any copyhold, his wife living, then she ought to come to the next Court or Law-day to make her claim and election, whether she will pay a penny and hold for her widow's estate, or pay half her husband's fine, and to keep the copyhold tenement during her life.

"Custom 4. That the husband of any wife (as customary tenant of the said manor) dying, seized of any customary tenement within the said manor, is entitled to have such customary tenement of his wife so dying, during his life, though the said husband had no issue of the body of his said wife.

"Custom 5. That if any copyholder or customary tenant of the said manor die, and leave his heir within the age of fourteen years, that then the nearest of kin and farthest from the land, have had, and ought to have the guardianship and custody of the body of such heir and his copyholds, held of that manor, so that at the next Court or Law-day he come in and challengeth the same, and to keep the same until the heir come to be of the age of fourteen years.

"Custom 6. That the heir of any customary tenant within the said manor is compellable to pay his fine to the lord of the said manor, and be admitted tenant before he attain his age of one and twenty years, if he come to the possession of his customary estate.

"Custom 7. That the fine due to the lord of the said manor upon the admission or alienation of any customary tenant, to any customary tenement within the said manor, is, and time out of mind was, double the quit-rent of the said customary tenement; that is to say, when the quit-rent of any customary tenement was twenty shillings, the tenant of such tenement did pay to the lord of the said manor forty shillings for a fine.

"Custom 8. That every heir and tenant of any customary lands of the said manor may sell his inheritance during the life of the widow of his ancestor, who enjoys such customary estate for life.

"Custom 9. That it is lawful for any of the copyholders or customary tenants of the said manor, to let her, his, or their copyholds for one year, but not for any longer term, without a licence from the lord of the said manor.

"Custom 10. 'That no certain fine is payable to the lord of the said manor from any customary tenant of the said manor for a licence to let his customary tenement; but such fine may exceed a penny in the pound of the yearly value of such customary tenement.

"Custom 11. That every copyholder of inheritance of the said manor may sell any of his coppices, under-woods, and rows, and use them at pleasure; and may dig for stone, coal, earth, marle, chalk, sand and gravel in their own grounds, to be employed thereon; and may also dig any of the commons or wastes belonging to the said manor for earth or gravel in the ancient pits there, where their predecessors have done, for the improvement of their copyholds.

"Custom 12. That all the customary tenants of the said manor, when and as often as their old pits, where they used to dig earth, marle, chalk, sand, clay, gravel, and other mould, were deficient, and would not yield the same for them, that they, the said customary tenants, may and have used to dig new pits in any of the wastes and commons of the lord within the said manor, and there dig and carry away earth, marle, chalk, sand, clay, gravel, and other mould at their pleasure, for the improvement of their customary tenements, or for other necessary uses, without the licence of the lord of the said manor.

"Custom 13. That the ancient customary tenants of the said manor (other than such as hold only purpresture lands) have always had common of pasture and feedings in all the lord's commons belonging to the said manor, viz. upon Cranbury Common, Hiltingbury Common, Ampfield Common, Bishop's Wood, Pit Down, and Merdon Down, for all their commonable cattle, levant and couchant, upon their respective copyhold tenements, within the said manor.

"Custom 14. That no customary tenant of the said manor can or ought to plough any part of the land upon the aforesaid wastes and commons, to lay dung, or for improving their customary lands.

"Custom 15. That the Customary tenants of the said manor have not had, nor ought to have in every year, at all times of the year, common of pasture in the wastes, heaths, and commons of the lord of the said manor within the said manor, for all their commonable cattle, without number or stint, exclusive of the lord of the said manor.

"Custom 16. That the hazels, furzes, maples, alders, wythies, crab-trees, fern, and bushes, growing upon the aforesaid wastes and commons, or in either of them, as also the acorns when they there fall, do belong to the customary tenants of the said manor, not excluding the lord of the said manor for the time being from the same. And that the customary tenants of the said manor have had, and used and ought to have, right of cutting furzes growing upon the wastes and commons of the said manor for their firing, and to cut fern for their uses and that the said customary tenants, in like manner, have right of cutting thorns, bushes, wythies, hazels, maples, alders, and crab-trees, growing upon the wastes and commons of the said manor, or in either of them, for making and repairing their hedges and fencing of their grounds, but they are not to commit any waste to the prejudice of the breeding, nursing, and raising of young trees of oak, ash, and beech, which do wholly belong to the lord of the said manor, to have, use, and fell; and that the acorns, after they are fallen, do wholly belong to the customary tenants of the said manor.

"Custom 17. That the customary tenants of the said manor have right to feed their cattle in the three coppices called South Holmes, Hele Coppice, and Holman Coppice, within the said manor, and a right to the mast there.

"Custom 18. That the lord of the said manor ought not to cut down the said coppices, or one of them altogether, or at any one time, but by parts or pieces, when he pleases.

"Custom 19. That when the lord of the said manor doth cut down any, or either of the said coppices, he, by the custom, is not compellable to fence the same for seven years after such cutting, nor to suffer the same to lie open.

"Custom 20. That neither Thomas Colson, William Watts, alias Watkins, nor the customary tenants of the tenement called Field House, have a right of selling or disposing sand in any of the wastes or commons of the lord of the said manor within the said manor.

"Custom 21. That any customary tenant of the said manor seized of any estate of inheritance, in any customary tenement within the said manor, may cut timber, or any other trees standing or growing in or upon his said customary tenement, for repairs of his ancient customary messuages, with their appurtenances, and for estovers and other necessary things to be used upon such his customary tenement, without the licence or assignment of the lord of the said manor, but not for building new messuages for habitation.

"Custom 22. That no customary tenant of the said manor can cut, sell, or dispose of any trees growing upon his customary tenement, without the licence of the lord of the said manor, unless for repairs, estovers, and other necessary things to be used upon his customary tenement.

"Custom 23. That any tenant seized of any estate of inheritance in any of the customary tenements of the said manor, may cut down timber trees or other trees, standing or growing in or upon one of his customary tenements, to repair any other of his customary tenements, within the said manor.

"Custom 24. That no tenant of any customary tenement of the said manor, may cut any timber trees or any other trees from off his customary tenement, nor give or dispose of the same, for repairing of any customary tenement, or any other customary tenement within the said manor.

"Custom 25. That the said customary tenants, and every of them, may cut down any old trees, called decayed pollard trees, standing or growing in or upon his customary tenement, and sell and dispose of the same, at his and their will and pleasure.

"Custom 26. That the lord of the said manor for the time being, when, and as often as his mansion-house and the outhouses called Merdon Farm House, shall want necessary repairs, may cut, and hath used to cut down, one timber tree from off one farm or customary tenement, once only during the life of the customary tenant of such one farm, or customary tenement, for the necessary repairs of the mansion-house and outhouses called Merton Farm House.

"Custom 27. That the lord of the said manor, for the time being, cannot cut down more trees than one, from any one customary tenement in the life-time of any customary tenant thereof, for the repairs aforesaid, nor can he take the loppings, toppings, boughs, or bark of such trees so by him cut down, nor can he carry the same away.

"Custom 28. That upon any surrender made before the reeve or beadle, with two customary tenants of the said manor, or before any two customary tenants of the said manor without the reeve or beadle, no herriot is due to the lord of the said manor, if the estate thereby made and surrendered be from the right heir.

"Custom 29. That by the custom of the said manor, the jury at the Court or Law-day held for the said manor, have yearly used to choose the officers of and for the said manor, for the year ensuing, viz. a Reeve, a Beadle, and a Hayward, and such officers have used, and ought to be sworn at the said Court, to execute the said offices for one year until they are lawfully discharged.

"Custom 30. That the Hayward's office hath been to collect and pay to the lord of the said manor such custom money as was agreed for in lieu of the custom works."

The boundaries of the manor of Merdon, including Cranbury, and up to the brook at Chandler's Ford, have been kept up by "progresses" round them. Probably the "gang" or Rogation procession was discontinued by either Sir Philip Hobby or Richard Maijor; but on the borders between Hursley and Baddesley, at a spot called High Trees Corner, near the railway, is marked in the old map, "Here stode Gospell Oke." It is not far from Wool's Grave, the next corner towards the Baddesley road. There, no doubt, the procession halted for the reading of the Gospel for Rogation week.

There are two curious entries in the old accounts:-

Chirurchets vi Hennes and Cockes as apereth

in the old customary which I had from John

Seymour.

And in the old book of Fines written in 1577 -

The Reve doth gather by his scores - £37 18 2.

The Bedell gathers the escheats.

The Reve the rents and eggs and is keeper of the West heth.

A small farm near the church was held by Corpus Christi College, Oxford, having probably been granted by Bishop Richard Fox, the founder, who held the See of Winchester from 1500 to 1528. The bearing in his coat of arms was a "pelican in her piety," and the Pelican was the name of the public house and of the farm that succeeded it down to the present day. The title as well as that of the college are of course connected with the emblem of the Pelican feeding her young from her own breast. Little pelicans, alternately with Tudor portcullises, profusely adorn Fox's chantry in Winchester Cathedral.

CHAPTER VI - CRANBURY AND BRAMBRIDGE

Great changes began at the Restoration. Robert Maunder became vicar of Hursley in 1660, on whose presentation is unknown; but that he or his curate were scholars is probable, since the entries in the parish registers both of Hursley and Otterbourne begin to be in Latin. Cranbury had passed from Dean Young to his brother Major General Young, and from him to his daughter, the wife or Sir Charles Wyndham, son of Sir Edmund Wyndham, Knight Marshall of England and a zealous cavalier. Brambridge, closely bordering on Otterbourne, on the opposite side of the Itchen, though in Twyford Parish, was in the possession of the Welles family. Brambridge and Otterbourne are divided from one another by the river Itchen, a clear and beautiful trout stream, much esteemed by fishermen. In the early years of Charles II. a canal was dug, beside the Itchen, for the conveyance of coal from Southampton. It was one of the first formed in England, and for two hundred years was constantly used by barges. The irrigation of the meadows was also much benefited, broad ditches being formed - "water carriages" as they are locally called - which conduct the streams in turn over the grass, so that even a dry season causes no drought, but they always lie green and fresh while the hills above are burnt brown.

Another work was set in hand during the reign of Charles II., namely the palace he designed to build in rivalry of Versailles. Sir Christopher Wren was the architect. The grounds were intended to stretch over the downs to a great distance, and on the highest point was to stand a pharos, whose light would be visible from the Solent. Fountains were to be fed from the Itchen, and a magnificent palace was actually begun, the bricks for it being dug from a clay pit at Otterbourne, which has ever since borne the name of Dell Copse, and became noted for the growth of daffodils. The king lodged at Southampton to inspect the work, and there is a tradition (derived from Dean Rennell) that being an excellent walker, he went on foot to Winchester. One of his gentlemen annoyed him by a hint to the country people as to who he was, whereupon a throng come out to stare at him, at one of the bridges. He escaped, and took his revenge by a flying leap over a broad "water carriage," leaving them to follow as they could.

His death put an end to his design, when only one wing of the building was completed. It was known as "the King's House" and was used as barracks till 1892, when it was unfortunately burnt to the ground.

Boyat, or Bovières, as it once was called, had been a "hundred," and was probably more of a village than at present, since up to 1840 there was a pound and stocks opposite to the single farm-house that remained. The lands stretched from the hill to the river, near which was a hamlet called Highbridge, just on the boundary between Twyford and Otterbourne. Here was an endowed Roman Catholic chapel, a mere brick building, at the back of a cottage, only distinguished by a little cross on the roof. There is reason to think that a good many dependants of the Brambridge family lived here, for there are entries in the parish register that infants had been born at Highbridge, but the curate of Otterbourne could not tell whether they had been baptized.

A new parchment parish register was provided in 1690, and very carefully kept by the curate, John Newcombe, who yearly showed it up to the magistrates at the Petty Sessions, when it was signed by two of them. A certain Augustin Thomas was a man of some property, comprising a house and two or three fields, which were known as "Thomas's Bargain," till one was used as a site for the Vicarage. Several surnames still extant in the parish are found in the register, Cox, Comley, Collins, Goodchild, Woods, Wareham - Anne and Abraham were the twin children of John and Anne Diddams, a curious connection with the name Didymus (twin), which seems to be the origin.

There must have been extensive repairs, if such they may be called, of the church, probably under the influence of Sir Charles and Lady Wyndham - for though Cranbury House stands in Hursley parish, it is so much nearer to

Otterbourne that the inhabitants generally attend the church there, - and two huge square pews in the chancel, one lined with red baize, the other bare, were appropriated to Cranbury, and might well have been filled by the children of Sir Charles and Dame James his wife - Jacoba in her marriage register at Hursley - for they had no less than seventeen children, of whom only five died in infancy, a small proportion in those days of infant mortality. The period of alteration is fixed by a great square board bearing the royal arms, with the initials W. and M. and the date 1687. No notice was taken of the Nassau shield, and indeed it must have been put up in a burst of enthusiasm for the glorious Revolution, for the lion, as best he can be recollected, had a most exultant expression, with his tongue out of one side of his mouth.

The black-letter Commandments on the chancel arch were whitewashed out, and a tablet in blue with gold lettering erected in their stead on each side of the altar. The east window had either then or previously been deprived of all its tracery, and was an expanse of plain glass with only a little remains of a cusp at the top of the arch. The bells were in one of the true Hampshire weather-boarded square towers, of which very few still exist in their picturesqueness. There were the remains of an old broken font, and a neat white marble one, of which the tradition was that it was given by a parish clerk named David Fidler, and it still exists as the lining of the present font.

Sir Charles Wyndham died in 1706, his wife in 1720. A small monument was raised for them in Hursley Church, with an inscription on a tablet now in the tower, purporting that the erection was by their daughters, Frances White and Beata Hall.

Frances was married to a man of some note in his day, to judge by the monument she erected to his memory in Milton Church, near Lymington, where his effigy appears, an upright figure cut off at the knees, and in addition to the sword in his hand there is a metal one, with a blade waved like a Malay crease, by the side of the monument. The inscription is thus -

THOMAS WHITE Esq., son of

IGNATIUS WHITE Esq. of Fiddleford in Dorsetshire.

He served three kings and Queen Ann as a Commander in the guards, and was much wounded. He was in the wars of Ireland and Flanders.

He had one son who dyed before him. He departed this life on the 17th of February in the year 1720.

This monument was erected by his widow Frances, one of the daughters of Sir Charles Wyndham, in the county of Southampton.

Mrs. White thus lost her husband and her mother in the course of the same year. Her brother sold the Cranbury property to Jonathan Conduitt, Esquire, who was a noted person in his day. He married Catherine Barton, the favourite niece and adopted daughter of Sir Isaac Newton. It may be remembered that this great man was a posthumous child, and was bred up by his mother's second husband, Barnabas Smith, Rector of North Witham, Lincolnshire, so as to regard her children as brothers and sisters. Hannah Smith married one Thomas Barton of Brigstock, and her daughter Catherine (whose name mysteriously is found as suing for the price of property sold to Charles II. for the site of the King's house at Winchester), lived with Sir Isaac Newton, was very beautiful, and much admired by Lord Halifax for her wit and gaiety. It was even reported that she was privately married to him, but this of course was mere scandal, and she became the wife of Jonathan Conduitt, educated at Trinity College, a friend and pupil of Newton, who had for many years assisted in the harder work of Master of the Mint, and wrote an essay on the gold and silver coinage of the realm. He was member of Parliament for Southampton. Sir Isaac made his home with his niece and her husband till his death in 1727, when Mr. Conduitt succeeded to his office as Master of the Mint, and intended to write his life, but was prevented by death in 1737. Among the materials which Mr. Conduitt had preserved is the record of Newton's saying, "I do not know what I may appear to the world, but to myself I seem to have been only like a boy playing on the sea shore, and diverting myself in now and then finding a smoother pebble or a prettier shell than ordinary, while the great ocean of truth lay all undiscovered before me."

A very curious relic of Sir Isaac survives in the garden at Cranbury Park, viz. a sun-dial, said to have been calculated by Newton. It is in bronze, in excellent preservation, and the gnomon so perforated as to form the cypher I. C. seen either way. The dial is divided into nine circles, the outermost divided into minutes, next, the hours, then a circle marked "Watch slow, Watch fast," another with the names of places shown when the hour coincides with our noonday, such as Samarcand and Aleppo, etc., all round the world. Nearer the centre are degrees, then the months divided into days. There is a circle marked with the points and divisions of the compass, and within, a diagram of the compass, the points alternately plain and embossed.

There is no date, but the maker's name, John Rowley, and the arms of Mr. Conduitt, as granted in 1717. Quarterly 1st and 4th Gules, on a fesse wavy argent, between three pitchers double eared or, as many bees volant proper.

2nd and 3rd Gules, a lion rampant argent between six acorns or. Impaling argent 3 boars' heads sable for Barton.

Crest - Two Caducean rods with wings, lying fesse ways or. Thereon a peacock's head, erased proper.

The motto - "Cada uno es hijo de sus obras." "Each one is son of his deeds" - translates the Spanish.

The 1st and 3rd quartering belongs to the old family of Chenduite, from which Jonathan Conduitt may have been descended. Probably he could not prove his right to their Arms, and therefore had the fresh grant.

Mr. Conduitt died in 1737, leaving a daughter, whose guardians sold Cranbury to Thomas Lee Dummer, Esquire, from whom it descended in 1765 to his son of the same name.

Catherine Conduitt married the son of Viscount Lymington, afterwards created Earl of Portsmouth.

CHAPTER VII - THE BUILDING AT HURSLEY

In the year 1718, Hursley was sold by Cromwell's two surviving daughters for £36,000 to William Heathcote, Esq., afterwards created a baronet.

The Heathcotes belonged to a family of gentle blood in Derbyshire. Gilbert Heathcote, one of the sons, was an Alderman at Chesterfield, and was the common ancestor of the Rutland as well as the Hursley family. His third son, Samuel, spent some years as a merchant at Dantzic, where he made a considerable fortune, and returning to England, married Mary the daughter of William Dawsonne of Hackney. He was an intimate friend of the great Locke, and assisted him in his work on preserving the standard of the gold coin of the realm. He died in 1708, his son William and brother Gilbert attained to wealth and civic honours.

Sir Gilbert was Lord Mayor in 1711 and was the last who rode in procession on the 9th of November. Both were Whigs, though the Jacobite Lord Mayor, whose support was reckoned on by the Stuarts, was their cousin.

At about twenty-seven years of age, William Heathcote married Elizabeth, only daughter of Thomas Parker, Earl of Macclesfield, and had in course of time six sons and three daughters. He was M.P. first for Buckingham and afterwards for Southampton. He was created a baronet in 1733.

There were plans drawn for enlarging the old lodge in which the Hobbys and Cromwells had lived, but these seem to have been found impracticable, and it was decided to pull the house down and erect a new one on a different site. Tradition, and Noble in his Cromwell, declared that the change was from dislike of the Cromwell opinions and usurpations, but Mr. Marsh considers this "mean and illiberal" and combats it sharply.

The new and much more spacious building was placed a little higher up on the hill, with a wide bowling-green on the south side, where in dry summers the old foundations of the former house can be traced, the walnut avenues leading up to it. The house was in the style that is now called Queen Anne, of red brick quoined with stone, with large-framed heavy sash windows and double doors to each of the principal rooms, some of which were tapestried with Gobelin arras representing the four elements - Juno, with all the elements of the air; Ceres presiding over the harvest, for the earth; Vulcan with the emblems of fire; and Amphitrite drawn by Tritons personifying water.

There was then a great central entrance-hall, in the middle of the northern side of the house, with stone steps going up at each end, outside, but, as we see from drawings and prints of the time, with no carriage-approach to the house, so that people must have driven up to the front door over the grass.

Sir William died in 1751, fifty-eight years old. His son, Sir Thomas, born in 1721, was the builder of old Hursley Church, which was begun in 1752, and completed the next year, only the tower being left of the former edifice. In 1808 some few capitals of the old pillars remained in parts of the village, and were adjudged by Mr. Marsh to be Saxon. It was said that the inside was very dark, the ground outside being nearly on a level with the windows, and six or eight steps descending to the floor.

It was all swept away, and the new structure was pronounced by Mr. Marsh to be exceedingly "neat, light, and airy." It was 82 feet long, and 49 broad, with two aisles, and an arched ceiling, supported on pillars. It might well be light, for the great round-headed windows were an expanse of glass, very glaring in sunshine, though mitigated by the waving lime-trees. The plan and dimensions followed those of the old church, and were ample enough, the north aisle a good deal shorter than the chancel, and all finished with gables crow-stepped in the Dutch fashion. It was substantially paved within, and was a costly and anxiously planned achievement in the taste of the time, carefully preserving all the older monuments. A mausoleum in the same style was built for the Heathcote family in the south-western corner of the churchyard, and gradually the white-washed walls of the church became ornamented (?) with the hatchments of each successive baronet and his wife, the gentlemen's shields with the winged globe as crest, and the motto Deus prosperat justos; the ladies' lozenge finished with a death's head above, and Resurgam below.

Sir Thomas was twice married and had eight children. He died at sixty-five years of age on 29th of June 1787. He was succeeded by his eldest son, the second Sir William, who was born in 1746, and was member for the county in three Parliaments. He was a man of great integrity, humanity, and charity, very affable and amiable, and unassuming in his manners, "and he died as he had lived, fearing God." He married Frances, daughter and co-heiress of John Thorpe of Embley, and had seven children.

His eldest son, Sir Thomas, married the heiress of Thomas Edwards Freeman, of Batsford, Gloucestershire, in 1799, and was known as Sir Thomas Freeman

Heathcote. He was member for the county from 1808 till 1820, when he retired. He is reported to have known an old man who said he had held a gate open for Oliver Cromwell, but this must have meant the grandson, who died in 1705.

Sir Thomas died without issue in his fifty-sixth year on the 21st day of February 1825.

CHAPTER VIII - OLD OTTERBOURNE

Thomas Dummer, Esquire, who in 1765 succeeded his father in the possession of Cranbury, was a man to whom some evil genius whispered, "Have a taste," for in 1770 he actually purchased the City Cross of Winchester to set it up at Cranbury, but happily the inhabitants of the city were more conservative than their corporation, and made such a demonstration that the bargain was annulled, and the Cross left in its proper place. He consoled himself with erecting a tall lath and plaster obelisk in its stead, which was regarded with admiration by the children of the parish for about sixty years, when weather destroyed it.

He also transported several fragments from Netley Abbey, which formed part of his property at Weston near Southampton, and set them up in his park as an object from the windows. There is an arch, the base of a pillar, and a bit of gateway tower, but no one has been able to discover the part whence they came, so that not much damage can have been done. The rear of the gateway has been made into a keeper's lodge, and is known to the village of Otterbourne as "the Castle."

He is also said to have had a kind of menagerie, and to have been once in danger from either a bear or a leopard; the man at Hursley who rescued him did not seem in his old age to be clear which it was, though he considered himself to have a claim on the property.

It would not have been easy to substantiate it, for Mr. Dummer died without heirs about 1790, leaving his property at Cranbury and Netley first to his widow, and after her to the Chamberlayne family.

Mrs. Dummer lived many years after her husband, and married an artist, then of some note, Sir Nathanael Dance, who assumed the name of Holland, and in 1800 was created a baronet. He threw up painting as a profession, but brought several good pictures to Cranbury. His wife survived him till 1823-24, when William Chamberlayne, M.P. for Southampton, came into the property, and from him, in 1829, it descended to his nephew, Thomas Chamberlayne, Esquire.

Brambridge had a more eventful history. From the Welleses, it passed to the Smythes, also Roman Catholics. Walter Smythe, the first of these, was second son of Sir John Smythe of Acton Burnell in Derbyshire. His daughter Mary Anne was married at nineteen to one of the Welds of Lulworth Castle, who died within a year, and afterwards to Thomas Fitzherbert, who left her a childless widow before she was twenty-five.

It was six years later that, after vehement passionate entreaties on the part of George, Prince of Wales, and even a demonstration of suicide, she was wrought upon to consent to a private marriage with him, which took place on the 21st of December 1785, at her house in Park Lane, the ceremony being performed by a clergyman of the Church of England, in the presence of her uncle and one of her brothers.

So testifies Jesse in his Life of George III. Nevertheless there is at Twyford a belief that the wedding took place at midnight in the bare little Roman Catholic Chapel at Highbridge, and likewise in Brambridge House, where the vicar officiated and was sworn to secrecy. The register, it is said, was deposited at Coutts's Bank under a lock with four keys. The connection with Twyford was kept up while the lady lived, but no one remains who can affirm the facts. Her first marriage, in early youth, was most probably, as described, at Brambridge. Her very small wedding ring is also extant, but neither ring nor ceremony can belong to her royal marriage. It would be curious that the adjoining parish of Marwell likewise had to boast (if that is a right word) of Henry VIII.'s marriage with Jane Seymour.

Mrs. Fitzherbert certainly visited Brambridge, for an old gardener named Newton, and Miss Frances Mary Bargus, who came to live at Otterbourne in 1820, remembered her, and the latter noted her fine arched brows. George IV.'s love for her was a very poor thing, but she was the only woman he ever had any real affection for, and he desired that her miniature should be buried with him.

She survived him for many years, and died in 1837 at eighty-one years old.

Her brother Walter was one of the English who visited Paris and was made prisoner by Napoleon I. at the rupture of the peace of Amiens, and detained till 1814. While he was a prisoner, his brother Charles caused all the limes in the avenue at Brambridge to be pollarded, and sold the tops for gun stocks. Nevertheless the trees are still magnificent, making three aisles, all the branches inwards rising up perpendicularly, those without sweeping gracefully down, and all budding and fading simultaneously. The pity is that the modern house should not have been built at one end or the other, so that they form actually a passage that leads to nothing. Since his death, the property has been sold, and has passed into strangers' hands. The endowment of the chapel has been transferred to one at Eastleigh, and the house to which it was attached belongs to a market garden.

The two parishes were near enough to the coast to be kept in anxiety by the French schemes for landing. The tenant of the Winchester College property at Otterbourne is said to have kept all her goods packed up, and to have stirred the fire with a stick all through one winter; and as late as between 1840-50, Mr. Bailey of Hursley still had in his barn the seats that had been prepared to fit into the waggons that were to carry the women into the downs in the event of a battle.

The Rev. John Marsh, who in 1808 collected the memoranda of Hursley and dedicated them to Sir William Heathcote, was curate of Hursley and incumbent of Baddesley. The Vicar was the Rev. Gilbert Heathcote, fifth son of Sir Thomas, second Baronet. He was afterwards Archdeacon of Winchester and a Canon of Winchester. He was a man of great musical talent, and some of his chants are still in use. The only other fact recollected of him was, that being told that he used hard words in his sermons, he asked a labourer if he knew what was meant by Predestination, and was answered, "Yes, sir, some'at about the innards of a pig." He generally resided there. Mr. Marsh remained curate of Hursley and was presented to the living of Baddesley. All this time Otterbourne had only one Sunday service, alternately matins or evensong, and the church bell was rung as soon as the clergyman could be espied riding down the lane. Old customs so far survived that the congregation turned to the east in the Creed, always stood up, if not sooner, when "Alleluia" occurred at the end of the very peculiar anthems, and had never dropped the response, "Thanks be to Thee, O Lord," at the end of the Gospel.

The Holy Communion was celebrated four times a year, 3s. 7d. being paid each time for the Elements, as is recorded in beautiful writing in "the Church Raiting book," which began to be kept in 1776. "Washan the surples" before Easter cost 4s.; a Communion cloth, tenpence; and for washing and marking it, sixpence. A new bell cost £ 5: 5: 10, and its "carridge" from London 11s. 10d. Whitewashing the church came to £1: 1s., and work in the gallery to 10s. 4d. Besides, there was a continual payment for dozens of sprow heads, also for fox heads at threepence apiece, for a badger's head, a "poul cat," marten cats, and hedgehogs. These last, together with sparrows, continue to appear till 1832, when the Rev. Robert Shuckburgh, in the vestry, protested against such use of the church rate, and it was discontinued. Mr. Shuckburgh was the first resident curate at Otterbourne, being appointed by the Archdeacon. He was the first to have two services on Sunday, though still the ante-Communion service was read from the desk, and he there pulled off his much iron-moulded surplice from over his gown and ascended the pulpit stair. The clerk limped along the aisle to the partitioned space in the gallery to take part in the singing.

But changes were beginning. The direct coaching road between Winchester and Southampton had been made, and many houses had followed it. The road that crosses Colden Common and leads to Portsmouth was also made about the same time, and was long called Cobbett's road, from that remarkable self-taught peasant reformer, William Cobbett, who took part in planning the direction.

Cobbett was a friend of Mr. Harley, a retired tradesman who bought the cottage that had belonged to a widow, named Science Dear, and enlarged it. Several American trees were planted in the ground by Cobbett, of which only one survives, a hickory, together with some straggling bushes of robinia, which Cobbett thought would make good hedges, being very thorny, and throwing up suckers freely, but the branches proved too brittle to be useful. About 1819 Mr. Harley sold his house and the paddock adjoining to Mary Bargus, widow of the Rev. Thomas Bargus, Vicar of Barkway in Hertfordshire, and she came to live there with her daughter Frances Mary. In 1622, Miss Bargus married William Crawley Yonge, youngest son of the Rev. Duke Yonge, Vicar of Cornwood, Devon, of the old family of Yonges of Puslinch. He then retired from the 52nd regiment, in which he had taken part in the Pyrenean battles, and in those of Orthez and Toulouse, and had his share in the decisive charge which completed the victory of Waterloo. They had two children, Charlotte Mary, born August 11th, 1823, and Julian Bargus, born January 31st, 1830.

CHAPTER IX - CHURCH BUILDING

A new era began in both Hursley and Otterbourne with the accession of Sir William Heathcote, the fifth baronet, and with the marriage of William Yonge.

Sir William was born on the 17th of May 1801, the son of the Rev. William Heathcote, Rector of Worting, Hants, and Prebendary of the Cathedral of Winchester, second son of Sir William, third baronet. His mother was Elizabeth, daughter of Lovelace Bigg Wither of Manydown Park in the same county. She was early left a widow, and she bred up her only son with the most anxious care. She lived chiefly at Winchester, and it may be interesting to note that her son remembered being at a Twelfth-day party where Jane Austen drew the character of Mrs. Candour, and assumed the part with great spirit.

He was sent first to the private school of considerable reputation at Ramsbury in Wiltshire, kept by the Rev. Edward Meyrick, and, after four years there, became a commoner at Winchester College, where it is said that he and Dr. William Sewell were the only boys who jointly retarded the breaking out of the rebellion against Dr. Gabell, which took place after their departure. However, in April 1818 he left Winchester, and became a commoner of Oriel

College, Oxford, where his tutor was the Rev. John Keble, only eight years older than himself, and not yet known to fame, but with an influence that all who came in contact with him could not fail to feel.

In 1821 Mr. Heathcote gained a First-class in his B.A. examination, and was elected Fellow of All Souls in November 1822. He began to read at the Temple, but in April 1825 he came into the property of his uncle, and in the November of the same year he married the Hon. Caroline Frances Perceval, the youngest daughter of Charles George Lord Arden. Both he and his wife were deeply religious persons, with a strong sense of the duties of their station. Education and influence had done their best work on a character of great rectitude and uprightness, even tending to severity, such as softened with advancing years. Remarkably handsome, and with a high-bred tone of manners, he was almost an ideal country gentleman, with, however, something of stiffness and shyness in early youth, which wore off in later years. In 1826 he became member for the county on the Tory interest.

As a landlord, he is remembered as excellent. His mother took up her abode at Southend House in Hursley parish, and under the auspices of the Heathcote family, and of the Misses Marsh, daughters of the former curate, Sunday and weekday schools were set on foot, the latter under Mrs. Ranger and her daughter, whose rule continued almost to the days of national education. One of his first proceedings was to offer the living of Hursley to the Rev. John Keble, who had spent a short time there as curate in 1826. It was actually accepted, when the death of a sister made his presence necessary to his aged father at Fairford in Gloucestershire; and for two years, during which the publication of the Christian Year took place, he remained in charge of a small parish adjacent to his home.

About 1824 Mrs. Yonge began to keep the first Sunday school at Otterbourne in a hired room, teaching the children, all girls, chiefly herself, and reading part of the Church Service to them at the times when it was not held at church. The only week-day school was on the hill, kept by a picturesque old dame, whose powers amounted to hindering the children from getting into mischief, but who - with the instinct Mrs. Charles describes - never forgave the advances that disturbed her monopoly.

In 1826, as Mrs. Yonge was looking at the empty space of a roadway that had led into the paddock before it became a lawn, she said, "How I should like to build a school here!"

"Well," said her mother, Mrs. Bargus, "you shall have what I can give."

Mrs. Yonge contrived the room built of cement, with two tiny ones behind for kitchen and bedroom for the mistress, and a brick floor; and the first mistress, Mrs. Creswick, was a former servant of Archdeacon Heathcote's.

She was a gentle woman, with dark eyes and a lame leg, so that she could not walk to church with the children, who sat on low benches along the nave, under no discipline but the long stick Master Oxford, the clerk, brandished over them. Nor could she keep the boys in any order, and the big ones actually kicked a hole nearly through the cement wall behind them. At last, under the sanction of the Rev. Gilbert Wall Heathcote, who had succeeded his father as Vicar of Hursley, a rough cast room was erected in the churchyard, where Master Oxford kept school, with more upright goodness than learning; and Mr. Shuckburgh, the curate, and Mr. Yonge had a Sunday school there.

The riots at the time of the Reform Bill did not greatly affect the two parishes, though a few villagers joined the bands who went about asking for money at the larger houses. George, Sir William's second son, told me that he remembered being locked into the strong room on some alarm, but whether it came actually to the point of an attack is a question. It was also said that one man at Otterbourne hid himself in a bog, that the rioters might not call upon him; and one other man, James Collins, went about his work as usual, and heard nothing of any rising.

One consequence of the riotous state of the country was the raising of troops of volunteer yeomanry cavalry. Charles Shaw Lefevre, Esq. (afterwards Speaker and Lord Eversley), was colonel, Sir William was major and captain of such a troop, Mr. Yonge a captain; but at one of the drills in Hursley Park a serious accident befell Sir William. His horse threw back its head, and gave him a violent blow on the forehead, which produced concussion of the brain. He was long in recovering, and a slight deafness in one ear always remained.

In 1835 a far greater trouble fell on him in the death of the gentle Lady Heathcote, leaving him three sons and a daughter. In the midst of his grief, he was able to bring his old friend and tutor nearer to him. Mr. Keble at the funeral gave him the poem, as yet unpublished,

I thought to meet no more,

which had been written after the funeral of his own sister, Mary Anne Keble. The elder Mr. Keble died in the course of the same year, and Mr. Gilbert Wall Heathcote, resigning the living to become a fellow of Winchester, it was again given to the Rev. John Keble. Mr. Heathcote had brought to Otterbourne a young Fellow of New College, a deacon just twenty-three, the Reverend William Bigg Wither, who came for six weeks and remained thirty-five years. He found only twelve Communicants in the parish, and left seventy!

Mr. Keble was already known and revered as the author of the Christian Year, and was Professor of Poetry at Oxford, when he came to Hursley; having married, on the 10th of October 1835, Charlotte Clarke, the most perfect of helpmeets to pastor or to poet, save only in the frailness of her health.

He had two years previously preached at Oxford the assize sermon on National Apostasy, which Newman marks as the beginning of the awakening of the country to church doctrine and practice. He and his brother were known as contributors to the Tracts for the Times, which were rousing the clergy in the same direction, but which were so much misunderstood, and excited so much obloquy, that Mr. Norris of Hackney, himself a staunch old-fashioned churchman, who had held up the light in evil times, said to his young friend, the Rev. Robert Francis Wilson, a first-class Oriel man, to whom the curacy of Hursley had been offered, "Now remember if you become Keble's curate, you will lose all chance of preferment for life."

Mr. Wilson, though a man of much talent, was willing to accept the probability, which proved a correct augury.

The new state of things was soon felt. Daily Services and monthly Eucharists, began; and the school teaching and cottage visiting were full of new life. Otterbourne had, even before Mr. Keble's coming, begun to feel the need of a new church. The population was 700, greatly overflowing the old church, so that the children really had to be excluded when the men were there. It was also at an inconvenient distance from the main body of the inhabitants, who chiefly lived along the high road. Moreover, the South Western Railway was being made, and passed so near, that to those whose ears were unaccustomed to the sound of trains, it seemed as if the noise would be a serious interruption to the service.

Mr. Yonge had begun to take measures for improving and enlarging the old church, but was recommended to wait for the appointment of the new incumbent. Mr. Keble threw himself heartily into the scheme, and it was decided that it would be far better to change the site of the church at once. The venerable Dr. Routh, who was then President of St. Mary Magdalen College, and used yearly to come on progress to the old manor house, the Moat House, to hold his court, took great interest in the project, and the college gave an excellent site on the western slope of the hill, with the common crossed by the high road in front, and backed by the woods of Cranbury Park. Also a subscription of large amount was given. Sir William Heathcote as patron, as well as Mr. Keble, contributed largely, and Mr. Bigg Wither gave up his horse, and presented £25 out of each payment he received as Fellow of New College. Other friends also gave, and, first and last, about £3000 was raised.

Church building was much more difficult in those days than in these. Ecclesiastical architecture had scarcely begun to revive, and experts were few, if any indeed deserved the title. An architect at Winchester, Mr. Owen Carter, was employed, but almost all the ideas, and many of the drawings of the details came from Mr. Yonge, who started with merely the power of military drawing (acquired before he was sixteen years old) and a great admiration for

York Cathedral.

The cruciform plan was at once decided on (traced out at first with a stick on Cranbury grand drive), but the slope of the ground hindered it from being built duly east and west; the material is brick, so burnt as to be glazed grey on one side. Hearing of a church (Corstan, Wiltshire) with a bell-turret likely to suit the means and the two bells, Mr. Yonge and Mr. Wither rode to see it, and it was imitated in the design. The chancel was, as in most of the new churches built at this time, only deep enough for the sanctuary, as surpliced choirs had not been thought possible in villages, and so many old chancels had been invaded by the laity that it was an object to keep them out.

Mr. Yonge sought diligently for old patterns and for ancient carving in oak, and in Wardour Street he succeeded in obtaining five panels, representing the Blessed Virgin and the four Latin Fathers, which are worked into the pulpit; also an exceedingly handsome piece of carving, which was then adapted as altar-rail - evidently Flemish - with scrolls containing corn and grapes, presided over by angels, and with two groups of kneeling figures; on one side, apparently an Emperor with his crown laid down, and the collar of the Golden Fleece around his neck, followed by a group of male figures, one with a beautiful face. On the other side kneels a lady, not an empress, with a following of others bringing flowers. At the divisions stand Religious of the four Orders, one a man. The idea is that it probably represents either the coronation of Maximilian or the abdication of Charles V. In either case there was no wife, but the crown is not imperial, and that is in favour of Maximilian. On the other hand the four monastic Orders are in favour of Charles V.'s embracing the religious life.

For the stone-work, Mr. Yonge discovered that the material chiefly used in the cathedral was Caen stone, though the importation had long ceased. He entered into communication with the quarrymen there, sent out a stone mason (Newman) from Winchester, and procured stone for the windows, reredos, and font, thus opening a traffic that has gone on ever since.

Mistakes were made from ignorance and lack of authoritative precedent, before ecclesiology had become a study; but whatever could be done by toil, intelligence, and self-devotion was done by Mr. Yonge in those two years; and the sixty years that have since elapsed have seen many rectifications of the various errors. Even as the church stood when completed, it was regarded as an effort in the right direction, and a good example to church builders. The first stone was laid in Whitsun-week 1837 by Julian Bargus, Mr. Yonge's five-year-old son. A school for the boys was built on a corner of the ground intended as churchyard, and a larger room added to the girls', the expense being partly defrayed by a bazaar held at Winchester, and in part by Charlotte Yonge's first book, The Château de Melville, which people were good enough to buy, though it only consisted of French exercises and translations. The consecration took place on the 30th of July 1838, and immediately after daily matins were commenced. So that the Church of St. Matthew has never in sixty years been devoid of the voice of praise, except during casual absences. Most of the trees in the churchyard were planted by Mr. Bigg Wither, especially the great Sequoia, and the holly hedge around was grown by him from the berries of the first Christmas decoration, which he sowed in a row under the wall of the boys' school, and transplanted when large enough.

It was in 1839 that Mr. Keble published his Oxford Psalter, a work he had been engaged on for years, paying strict and reverent attention to the Hebrew original, and not thinking it right to interweave expressions of his own as guidance to meaning. His belief was that Holy Scripture is so many-sided, and so fathomless in signification, that to dwell on one point more than another might be a wrong to the full impression, and an irreverence in the translation. Thus, as a poet, he sacrificed a good deal to the duty of being literal, but his translation is a real assistance to students, and it is on the whole often somewhat like to Sternhold's, whom he held in much respect for his adherence to the originals.

Perhaps it may be mentioned here that the parishes of Hursley and Otterbourne were in such good order under the management of Sir William Heathcote and Mr. Yonge, that under the new Poor Law they were permitted to form a small Union of four, afterwards five, and now six parishes.

Ampfield was a hamlet lying on the western side of Hursley Park and wood, a very beautiful wood in parts, of oak and beech trees, which formed lovely vaulted arcades, one of which Mr. Keble used to call Hursley Cathedral. The place was increasing in population, and nearly two miles of woodland and park lay between it and the parish church.

Sir William Heathcote, therefore, resolved to build a church for the people, and Mr. Yonge was again the architect and clerk of the works, profiting by the experience gained at Otterbourne, so as to aim at Early English rather than Decorated style. A bell turret, discovered later at Leigh Delamere in Wiltshire, was a more graceful model than that of Corston. The situation was very beautiful, cut out, as it were, of the pine plantation on a rising ground above the road to Romsey, so that when the first stone was laid by Gilbert Vyvyan, Sir William's third son, the Psalm, "Lo, we heard of the same at Ephrata, and found it in the wood," sounded most applicable. St. Mark was the saint of the dedication, which fell opportunely on 21st April 1841, very near Mr. Keble's birthday, St. Mark's day, and to many it was a specially memorable day, as the Rev. J. H. Newman was present with his sister, Mrs. Thomas Mozley, and her husband, then vicar of Cholderton; and the Rev. Isaac Williams, a sacred poet, whose writings ought to be better known than they are, was also present. The endowment was provided by the chapter of Winchester giving up the great tithes, and a subscription of which T. White, Esq. of Ampfield gave £500.

The Rev. Robert Francis Wilson was the first curate, being succeeded in the curacy of Hursley by the Rev. Peter Young, then a deacon, who inhabited the old vicarage. The present one, which had been built by Sir Thomas Freeman Heathcote, was made over to the living by Sir William some years later.

Immediately after the consecration, Sir William was married to Selina, daughter of Evelyn John Shirley, Esq., of Eatington, Warwickshire, a marriage occasioning great happiness and benefit to all the parish and neighbourhood.

CHAPTER X - HURSLEY CHURCH

In one of his prose writings Mr. Keble speaks of the faithful shepherd going on his way though storms may be raging in the atmosphere; and such might be a description of his own course as regarded his flock, though there were several of these storms that affected him deeply. One gust came very near home.

The diocesan, Bishop Charles Sumner, was an excellent and conscientious man, with a much deeper sense of his duties as a bishop than his immediate predecessors, and of great kindness and beneficence; but he had been much alarmed and disturbed by the alleged tendencies of the Tracts for the Times, and shared in the desire of most of the authorities to discourage their doctrines and practice. When, therefore, the curate of Hursley came to Farnham to be admitted to the priesthood, he was required, contrary to the usual custom with candidates, to state categorically his views upon the Holy Eucharist. He used the expressions of the Catechism, also those of Bishop Ridley, but was desired to use his own individual words; and when these were sent in, he was rejected, though they did not outrun the doctrine that had always been taught by the close followers of the doctrine of the Catechism. Nevertheless, in spite of this disapproval, there was no withdrawal of his licence, and he remained at Hursley, not thinking it loyal to seek Ordination from another bishop, as would readily have been granted. He married Mrs. Keble's cousin, Miss Caroline Coxwell, and their young family was an infinite source of delight to the childless vicarage.

Their baby ways, to one who held that "where christened infants sport, the floor is holy," and who read a mystical meaning into many of their gestures and words, were a constant joy and inspiration; and there grew up a store of poems upon them and other little ones, especially the children of Dr. George Moberly, then headmaster of Winchester College (later bishop of Salisbury). These Mr. Keble thought of putting together for publication, being chiefly impelled to do so by the desire to improve Hursley Church, the eighteenth century arrangement of which really prevented the general inculcation of the more reverent observances which teach and imply doctrine.

In consideration of the feelings of certain old parishioners, and the other more pressing needs, as well as of the patience with which so great an enterprise needed in his mind to be contemplated, nine years had elapsed since his incumbency had begun before he wrote: "We are stirring about our Church, and next spring I hope really to go to work; you must come and see the plans first, or else hereafter for ever hold your peace in respect of alleging impediments. One feels that one's advanced age has not rendered one fitted to set about such works; but really the irreverence and other mischiefs caused by the present state of Hursley Church seem to leave one no choice."

The step that had first been taken was one for which many generations far and wide have reason to be grateful, the arrangement and publication of the Lyra Innocentium, to a certain degree on the lines of the Christian Year, so as to have one poem appropriated to each Sunday and holy day (though these were only fully marked off in a later edition).

The book is perhaps less universally read than the Christian Year, and is more unequal, some poems rising higher and into greater beauty, some deeper and showing that the soul had made further progress in these twenty years, some very simple in structure, fit for little children, yet with a grave and solemn thought in the last verse.

Those that are specially full of Hursley atmosphere, on events connected with the author, may be touched on here.

"Christmas Eve Vespers" was suggested by the schoolmaster's little daughter going into church before the decoration had been put up, and exclaiming, disappointed, "No Christmas!" "The Second Sunday in Lent" recalls, in the line on "the mimic rain on poplar leaves," the sounds made by a trembling aspen, whose leaves quivered all through the summer evenings, growing close to the house of Mr. Keble's life-long friend and biographer, Sir John Taylor Coleridge, at Ottery St. Mary. An engraving of Raffaelle's last picture "The Transfiguration" hung in the Vicarage drawing-room.

"The Fourth Sunday in Lent," on the offering of the lad with the five loaves, was suggested by the stained window on that subject given by the young Marquess of Lothian - a pupil for some years of Mr. Wilson at Ampfield - to the church at Jedburgh, built by his mother. Now that he has passed away, it may be remarked that he, as well as all the children commemorated in these poems, grew up so as to leave no painful impression connected with them. "Keep thou, dear boy, thine early vow," was fulfilled in him, as it was with George Herbert Moberly, the eldest son of Dr. Moberly, who, when a young child staying at the vicarage, was unconsciously the cause of the poems "Loneliness" and "Repeating the Creed," for Easter Sunday and Low Sunday. Frightened by unwonted solitude at bedtime, he asked to hear "something true," and was happy when Mrs. Keble produced the Bible. He was a boy of beautiful countenance, and his reverent, thoughtful look, as he repeated the Creed, delighted Mr. Keble. It was little expected then that he was doomed to a life-long struggle with invalidism, though he was able to effect much as a thinker and a priest before he, too, was taken to see in Paradise "the glorious dream around him burst."

It was a baby sister of his who drew herself up in her nurse's arms with a pretty gesture, like a pheasant's neck in a sort of reproof, as she said "Thank you" to her little self, when she had held out a flower to Mr. Keble, which, for once in his life, he did not notice; and his self-reproach produced the thoughts of thankfulness. One of the gems of the Lyra, "Bereavement," was the thought that came to the mind of the Pastor as he buried the little sister, the only child except the elder girl, of the bailiff at Dr. Moberly's farm. "Fire" embodied his feeling about a burnt child at Ampfield -

We miss thee from thy place at school

  And on thy homeward way,

Where violets, by the shady pool,

  Peep out so shyly gay

The Lullaby, with the view of the burnished cross upon the spire, and the girl singing the baby to sleep with the old Psalm -

In Thee I put my stedfast trust,

Defend me, Lord, for Thou art just,

is another Ampfield scene, inspiring noble and gentle thoughts for Innocents' Day.

"Lifting up to the Cross" (St. James's Day) was the product of a drawing brought home from Germany of a sight beheld by Miss Maria Trench, on a journey with Sir William and Lady Heathcote. She afterwards became Mrs. Robert F. Wilson, and made her first wedded home at Ampfield; and there is another commemoration of that journey in the fountain under the bank in Ampfield churchyard, an imitation of one observed in Tyrol and with the motto -

  While cooling waters here you drink

    Rest not your thoughts below,

  Look to the sacred sign and think

    Whence living waters flow,

Then fearlessly advance by night or day,

The holy Cross stands guardian of your way.

"More Stars" (All Saints' Day) and "Wakefulness" (The Annunciation) are reminiscences of Charles Coleridge Pode, a little nephew of Mr. Yonge, and his ecstatic joy on the first night of being out of doors late enough to see the glory of the stars. A few months later, on a sister being born, he hoped that her name would be Mary "because he liked the Virgin Mary." And when, only a few days later, his own mother was taken from him, he lay awake and silent, night after night. He, too, was one who fulfilled his early promise, till, as a young physician, he was cut off after much patient suffering. "More Stars" is also attributed to an exclamation of one of Mr. Peter Young's children; but in point of fact, most little ones have broken out in a similar joyous shout on their first conscious sight of the starry heavens.

Mrs. Keble used to forbear telling of the subjects of these poems, lest, as she said, there might be a sort of blight on the children in breaking the reserve; but most of them are beyond the reach of that danger in publicity; and I can only further mention that the village children en masse, and the curate's in detail, furnished many more of the subjects, while still they only regarded Mr. Keble as their best of playmates.

They cheered him when the great sorrow of his life befell him in the secession of John Henry Newman, hitherto his friend and fellow-worker. It came at a time when perhaps he was most fitted to bear it, when his brother in Gloucestershire and his wife at home had just begun to recover from a terrible typhoid fever caught at Bude.

Words spoken in the immediate prospect of death, by Mrs. Keble, strengthened her husband's faith and made him more than ever determined to hold fast by the Church of his fathers; and the thankfulness and exhilaration caused by the improvement in her health carried him the better over the first blow, though he went out alone to a quiet deserted chalk-pit to open the letter which he knew would bring the final news of the reception of his friend into the Roman Church.

Nor did his Hursley plans stand still. Under the management of Sir John Taylor Coleridge and other friends, the Christian Year had become much more profitable, and the Lyra also brought in a considerable quota, so that the entire work could be undertaken at Mr. Keble's expense.

It was decided, partly by Mr. Yonge himself, that the enterprise was on too large a scale for his partial knowledge, and moreover, much progress had been made during these nine years in ecclesiology, so that architects who had made it their study were to be found. The design was committed to William Harrison, Esq., a relation of Archdeacon Harrison, a very old friend and contemporary. It followed the lines of the existing church, which were found to be so solid and well built as for the most part only to need casing and not renewal, nor was the old tower taken down.

The contract with Locke and Nesham was for £3380, exclusive of the flooring, the wood-work, and other fittings of the interior. For this £1200 was set aside, but the sum was much exceeded, and there were many offerings from private friends.

The altar of cedar-wood was the gift of Robert Williams, Esq.; the altar plate was given by Mrs. Heathcote; the rails by the architect; the font by the Rev. William Butler and Emma his wife, and the clergy and sisters of Wantage. Mr. Butler was then vicar of Wantage, later canon of Worcester and dean of Lincoln. The present cedar credence table was made long after Mr. Keble's death, the original one was walnut, matching the chancel fittings.

This was proposed as the inscription on the base of the font, to be entirely hidden -

Ecclesiæ Parochiali

Sanctorum Omnium

In agro Hursleiense

Hunc Fontem, Lavacrum Regenerationis,

In honorem D. N. J. C.

Gratis animis

D.D.D.

Presbyteri, Diacones, Lectores, Sorores

Ecclesiæ SS. Petri et Pauli

Indigna familia

Apud Wantagium

Whether the whole was actually cut out on the under side of the granite step must be uncertain.

The steps of the sanctuary have in encaustic tiles these texts. On the lowest:

Blessed are they that do His commandments, that they may have a right to the Tree of Life, and enter through the gates into the city.

On the step on which the rails stand:

Blessed are they which do hunger and thirst after righteousness, for they shall be filled.

On the next:

Blessed are they that mourn, for they shall be comforted. Blessed are the pure in heart, for they shall see God.

And on the highest:

Thine eyes shall see the King in His beauty, they shall behold the land that is very far off.

The lectern was the offering of the friend of his youth, the Rev. Charles Dyson, Rector of Dogmersfield, copied from that at Corpus Christi College, where they first met.

The corbels were carefully chosen: those by the chancel arch are heads of St. Peter and St. Paul, as exponents of the inner mysteries; those by the east window are St. Athanasius and St. Augustine as champions of the faith. On the corbels of the north porch, looking towards the hills of Winchester, are Bishops Andrewes and Ken on the outside; on the inside, Wykeham and Waynflete. On the south porch, St. Augustine of Canterbury, and the Empress Helena over the door; on the outside, Bishop Sumner and Queen Victoria to mark the date of building.

"How would you like to have the book boards of the seats?" wrote the architect; "perhaps it would suggest the idea of a prayer desk if they were made to slope as the chancel stalls?"

And certainly their finials do suggest kneeling, and the arrangement is such that it is nearly impossible not to assume a really devotional attitude.

A stranger clergyman visited the church, measured the font and the height to the ceiling, and in due time, in 1850, there arrived the beautiful carved canopy, the donor never being known.

The windows did not receive their coloured glass at first; but Mr. Keble had an earnest wish to make them follow the wonderful emblematic series to which he had been accustomed in the really unique Church of Fairford, where he had grown up. The glass of these windows had been taken in a Flemish ship on the way to Spain by one John Tame, a Gloucestershire merchant, who had proceeded to rebuild his parish church so as fitly to receive it, and he must also have obtained the key to their wonderful and suggestive arrangement.

Fairford Church is much larger than Hursley, so that the plan could not be exactly followed, but it was always in Mr. Keble's mind. It was proposed that the glass should be given by the contribution of friends and lovers of the Christian Year. Two of the windows came from the Offertory on the Consecration day, one three-light was given by Mrs. Heathcote (mother of Sir William), another by Sir William and Lady Heathcote, one by the Marchioness of Bath, and one by the Marchioness of Lothian. The designs were more or less suggested by Dyce and Copley Fielding, but the execution was carried out by Wailes, under the supervision of Butterfield. The whole work was an immense delight to Mr. Keble, and so anxious was he that the whole should be in keeping, that the east window was actually put in three times before it was judged satisfactory. The plan of the whole was Mr. Keble's own; and though the colours are deeper, and what is now called more crude, than suits the taste of the present day, they must be looked upon with reverence as the outcome of his meditations and his great delight. I transcribe the explanation that his sister Elisabeth wrote of their arrangement:

The Hursley windows are meant to be a course of Instruction in Sacred History from Adam to the last day the church being dedicated to All Saints.

The north-west window has Adam and Noah. The windows along the north aisle each represent two persons from the Old Testament.

The three-light window on the north side, David with the ground plan of the Temple, Moses with the Tables of the Law, Solomon with the Model of the Temple. The Medallion under Moses is the Altar of Incense, and some of the Holy things.

The whole of that window means to represent the fixing and finishing of the Old Religion.

Then comes in the north chancel, Isaiah, Jeremiah, Ezekiel, and Daniel, the prophets preparing for the Gospel.

The north-east window has the Circumcision connecting the Law with the Church, with the figures of Anna and Simeon on each side.

East window: The Crucifixion, The Blessed Virgin and St. John on each side, The Agony, Bearing the Cross, and the Scourging.

The side window of the Sanctuary has St. Stephen and St. John the Baptist as the nearest Martyrs to our Lord, both before and after Him, and their martyrdoms underneath.

The south-east window: The Resurrection, with soldiers at the Sepulchre. St. Peter and St. Paul on each side.

The south chancel windows: The Four Evangelists; under, St. Luke, the Disciples at Emmaus; under, St. John, he and St. Peter at the Sepulchre.

The three-light south window: St. James the Less, first Bishop of Jerusalem; underneath, the Council in Acts x. 6. At his side two successors of the Apostles, St. Clement of Rome, Phil. iv. 3, and St. Dionysius of Athens, Acts xvii. 34, to show how the Church is built upon the Apostles.

In the west window, the Last Judgment, with St. Michael with his scales, and answering to Adam and Noah in the west window of the north aisle; and as a repentance window, St. Peter and St. Mary Magdalene in the west of the south aisle. In the two windows close to the font, St. Philip and Nicodemus, for baptism.

So were carried out the lines in the Lyra Innocentium.

> The Saints are there the Living Dead,
> The mourners glad and strong;
> This sacred floor their quiet bed,
> Their beams from every window shed
> Their voice in every song.

The clerestory windows were put in somewhat later, on finding that the church was dark, and Mr. Keble wished to have the children mentioned in Scripture, in outline upon them, but this was not carried out.

It was first thought probable that readers of the Christian Year and the Lyra Innocentium might have presented these stained windows, but the plan fell through, and the only others actually given were the repentance window, representing St. Peter and St. Mary Magdalene, by Mr. Harrison. Two were paid for by special offertories, and the rest were finally given by Mr. Keble, as the sums came in from his published writings.

The spire, completing the work, was added to the ancient tower by Sir William Heathcote.

The foundation stone, a brass plate with an inscription surrounded by oak leaves and acorns, was laid on the 29th of May 1847, but the spot is unknown. The entire cost, exclusive of the woodwork and the gifts mentioned, amounted to £6000. The large barn was used as a temporary church, and there are happy recollections connected with it and with the elm-shaded path between the Park and the vicarage field. When all sat on forms without the shade of pews, example taught a lesson of reverent attitude to the congregation, who felt obliged to lay aside any bad habits which might have grown up out of sight, so as to be unconsciously prepared for the new church, where the very width of the open benches and the shape of their ends are suggestive of kneeling in prayer. The period of the building was a time of enjoyment to Mr. Keble, for it was symbolical to him of the "edifying," building up, of the living stones of the True Church, and the restoring her waste places. When the workmen were gone home he used to walk about the open space in the twilight silence in prayer and meditation.

When the topmost stone was to be added, on 18th October 1848, and the weathercock finally secured, Mr. Keble ascended to the elevation that he might set his hand to the work, and there said a thanksgiving for the completion - "The hands of Zerubbabel have laid the foundation of this house. His hands shall also finish it" (Zech. iv. 9).

The day of the Consecration was an exceedingly happy one, on 24th October 1848, the only drawback being that Sir William Heathcote was too unwell to be present. There was a great gathering - the two Judges, Coleridge and Patteson, and many other warm and affectionate friends; and Sir John Coleridge was impressed by the "sweet state of humble thankfulness" of the Vicar and his wife in the completion of the work.

The sermon at Evensong on that day was preached by Mr. Keble himself, in which he spoke of the end of all things; and said the best fate that could befall that new church was that it should be burnt at the Judgment Day.

He thought, probably, of the perils of perversion from true Catholic principles which the course of affairs in these days made him dread exceedingly, and hold himself ready to act like the Non-jurors, or the Free Kirk men in Scotland, who had resigned all for the sake of principle. "Nevertheless," he wrote, "I suppose it is one's duty to go on as if all were encouraging."

And he did go on, and supported others till, by God's Providence, the tide had turned, and much was effected of which he had only dreamt as some day possible. It was in this frame of mind that the poem was composed of which this is a fragment:

The shepherd lingers on the lone hillside,

In act to count his faithful flock again,

Ere to a stranger's eye and arm untried

He yield the rod of his old pastoral reign.

He turns and round him memories throng amain,

Thoughts that had seem'd for ever left behind

O'ertake him, e'en as by some greenwood lane

The summer flies the passing traveller find,

Keen, but not half so sharp as now thrill o'er his mind.

For indeed every lapse in his parish turned to fill their pastor with self-blame.

CHAPTER XI - THE GOLDEN DAYS OF HURSLEY

Those forebodings of Mr. Keble's mercifully never were realised; many more years were granted in which Hursley saw the Church and the secular power working together in an almost ideal way.

To speak of what Sir William Heathcote was as a county gentleman would be difficult. He was for many years Chairman of the Quarter Sessions, and it is worth recording that when King Frederick William IV. of Prussia wished for information on the practical working of the English system of government, and sent over two jurists to enquire into the working of the unpaid magistracy, they were advised to attend the Winchester Quarter Sessions, as one of the best regulated to be found. They were guests at Hursley Park, and, as a domestic matter, their interest in English dishes, and likewise their surprise at the status of an English clergyman, were long remembered.

Considerable county undertakings originated in these days - a new and well-managed lunatic asylum at Fareham, a renewed jail on the then approved principles, and the inauguration of county police. In all these undertakings Sir William Heathcote and Mr. Yonge were active movers, and gave constant superintendence while they were carried out. Ill health obliged Sir William to retire from the representation of North Hants in the Conservative interest in 1847, but in 1854, on the recommendation of Sir Robert Harry Inglis, he was elected member for the University of Oxford, and so remained till his final retirement in 1868. What he was in both public and private capacities has nowhere been better expressed than by the late Earl of Carnarvon in a letter to the editor of the Times.

Long time a county member, and intimately acquainted with the subjects and interests which formed the heritage of English county gentlemen, he was, as a chairman of Quarter Sessions, recognised and often appealed to as the very representative and pattern of the class; and when afterwards he accepted the blue riband of Parliamentary representation as member for the University of Oxford, from first to last, through all the waves and weathers of political and personal bitterness, he retained the trust of friend and opponent. So long as he cared to keep that seat, all men desired to keep him. For this was his special characteristic, that in every period and pursuit of life, in the public business of his county, in the House of Commons, in the University, he not only enjoyed respect and affection, but he conciliated the confidence of all.

It was the unconscious tribute to a whole life and character. For to a remarkable clearness and vigour of intellect, he added a fairness of mind, a persuasiveness and courtesy of manner, with an inflexible uprightness of purpose, which won to him friend and stranger alike. I have never known any one who was not bettered by his converse, but I think none outside his own county and society can fully appreciate the remarkable influence which his name and character - in the later years it might be truly said "clarum et venerabile nomen" - exercised on all with whom he was connected. If indeed he had a fault, it was that his standard of action was so high, his nature so absolutely above the littleness of ordinary life, that he attributed to inferior men far purer and more unselfish objects than those that really moved them. "Vixit enim tanquam in Platonis politeia, non tanquam in Romuli faece."

It is the common fault of biographers to over-colour the character of a favourite hero, but those who knew Sir William Heathcote will admit that there is no exaggeration in what I have said. He was the highest product of a class and school of thought which is fast disappearing, and which will perhaps find few representatives in the next generation. With change of time comes also change of men; and the statesmen and politicians of the new world, whatever their merits or demerits, will probably be of a very different order from him of whom I am writing. The old university culture, the fastidious taste, the independence of thought, the union of political life with county associations - bound up as they are in this case by a rare intelligence and a moderation of mind which trimmed, with an almost judicial impartiality, the balance of thought on all matters submitted to him - are not a combination to be easily found in any age or society; but it may be safely predicted that they will be even less common in the coming age than they were in the generation of which Sir William Heathcote was a representative and ornament. Be this, however, as it may, I desire, by your favour, to record here the loss of one who deserved, if ever man did, the name of an English worthy.

This warm-hearted tribute is the exact truth, as all could testify who ever had occasion to ask Sir William's advice or assistance. Another such testimony must be added, from a speech of Lord Chief Justice Coleridge at Nobody's Club.

I looked at him from another point of view, and I can tell you only how he struck me, a man much younger, of different surroundings, differing from him in many opinions, political and religious. Yet it is my pride and sorrowful delight to recollect that Sir William Heathcote gave me his friendship for nearly forty years; and it is not presumptuous to say that his friendship deepened into affection. I could not say if I would, and I would not if I could, all that he was to me, how much of what is best (if there is any) in my life I owe to him, how much affection and reverence has gone with him to his grave. His house was open like another home; in joy, and still more in sorrow, his sympathy was always warm and ready, in trouble and in difficulty his advice was always at hand. What advice it always was! What comfort and strength there was in his company! For the time at least he lifted one up and made one better. Inflexible integrity, stern sense of duty, stainless honour, these qualities a very slight acquaintance with Sir William Heathcote at once revealed. But he had other great qualities too. He was one of the closest and keenest reasoners I ever knew. He was a man of the soundest and strongest judgment; and yet full of the most perfect candour and full of forbearance and indulgence for other men. And for a man of his intellect, and, indeed, for a man, he was wonderfully modest and shy, and of a humility which was, as I saw it, profoundly touching. Yet there was no weakness in him. Not unbecomingly, not one whit more than was just, he believed in himself, in his position, in his family; he had dignity true and inborn without the need of self-assertion, and love and respect towards him went hand in hand.

Mr. Keble once said, coming away from a long talk with him, that it was like holding intercourse with some old Christian knight. And so it was . . .

I am not one of those who believe in the degeneracy of the race, and I look forward to the future with hope rather than with dismay. I believe upon the whole the world improves. It is useless to be always looking back to be a laudator temporis acti se puero is placed by the wise and genial Horace to the discredit and not to the credit of old age. But I do think that each age has its own virtues, and its own type of excellence, and these do not return. We may have good things, but we shall not have the same good things. We shall have, I hope, good men, and great men, and noble men, in time to come, but I do not think we shall see again a Sir William Heathcote. That most charming mixture of dignified self respect, with unfailing gracious courtesy to others, those manners in which frankness and refinement mingled with and set off each other, that perfect purity of thought and utterance, and yet that thorough enjoyment of all that was good and racy in wit or humour - this has passed away with him. So beautiful and consistent a life in that kind of living we shall hardly see again.

He was preserved to our time to show us of a later age a perfect specimen of the old-fashioned, high-bred, highly cultivated county gentleman; and a finer type of Englishman it is hardly possible to conceive.

These two portraits, they are too true to be called eulogies, thoroughly describe Sir William as he was in friendship, as he was not only to his original contemporaries but to their sons, so that he came to be a generally looked up to father, as it were, to the magistracy of the county as well as the neighbourhood. A portrait of him by G. Richmond, Esq., R.A., was subscribed for by the magistracy and placed in the County Hall, which began to be newly restored under his auspices, so as worthily to show the work of Henry III. in the beautiful old banqueting hall.

Already, however, a great loss had been suffered in William Crawley Yonge, who had worked by his side in all his public undertakings, carrying out all that was done in a spirit of thoroughness that never rested till perfection had been attained as far as possible. His own parish of Otterbourne had felt his influence, and was noted for good order and improvement. Both Otterbourne and Hursley had land in allotments from at least 1830, long before the arrangement was taken up by Government. Mr. Yonge's strong churchmanship and deep religious feeling told on all around, and there was a strong sense of his upright justice, as much as his essential kindness. The end came suddenly; apoplexy brought on by the hurry and confusion of sending off his only son, Julian Bargus Yonge, in the Rifle Brigade to the Crimean War. He died on the

26th of February 1854. "What shall we do without him?" were the first words of Sir William Heathcote's letter to Mr. Keble on receiving the tidings.

It should be mentioned here that six young men from Otterbourne were concerned in the Crimean War - Captain Denzil Chamberlayne and Julian B. Yonge, though health obliged the latter to return from Varna, while the former took part in the famous Balaklava charge, and was unhurt, though his horse was killed. And four of the privates, John Hawkins, James and William Mason, and Joseph Knight, of whom only James Mason lived to return. An inscription built into the wall of the churchyard records their names, with the inscription, suggested by Mr. Keble, "It is good for a man that he bear the yoke in his youth."

And here William Yonge's daughter must record Sir William's never-failing kindness to her mother and herself, both in matters of business and in personal criticism, and assistance in those matters in her works in which the counsel of a man acquainted with the law is needful to prevent mistakes. Indeed, in the discussions on character and adventures, nothing was ever more evident to her than that she was talking (as Mr. Keble said) to a true specimen of the most pure-minded chivalry.

On 16th September 1868 Sir William retired from Parliament, and, on the 9th of August 1870, was sworn of the Privy Council. This appointment gave him the greater satisfaction as a testimony to his consistent integrity through his whole parliamentary career, as it came from the Gladstonian ministry, and he had been forced by his deep Church and State convictions to separate from Mr. Gladstone, the friend and fellow-worker of his younger days.

His last great public achievement was the rebuilding and improvement of the County Hospital. Winchester had been the first provincial city to possess a County Hospital, and the arrangements had grown antiquated and by no means accordant with more advanced medical practice. A subscription was raised, and with the warm co-operation of Warden Robert S. Barter of Winchester College, the present building was erected, on Mr. Butterfield's plans, in a more healthy and airy situation, in the year 1868, with a beautiful chapel for the nurses and patients, and with the modern system of nursing carried out. As was said, when in 1878 Sir William resigned the post of Chairman of the Committee, he was the father and the founder of the institution.

Few men have earned by a lifetime so much honour, gratitude, and affection as he by one consistent, upright course of life, or have left a nobler memory.

A few words we must give to the festivals. There was the yearly distribution of Christmas beef to all the labourers and artisans employed on the estate, and widows. There was occasionally a grand "beating of the bounds" of the Manor of Merdon, followed by a dinner in a tent to the tenants, at which the "Lord of the Manor" made a speech, hoping that in times to come the days of "the Old Sir William" might be kindly remembered; and somewhat later there were private theatricals, performed chiefly by the family, which were a great pleasure to friends and tenants.

What a centre of hospitality, cheerfulness, and kindness Hursley Park was in those days can hardly be described, though remembered by many as a sort of golden age of Hursley.

CHAPTER XII - HURSLEY VICARAGE

The Golden Age of Hursley did not deduce all its honour from the manor house. The vicarage was perhaps the true centre of the light which the Park reflected, or rather both knew that their radiance alike came from One Source above, in whose Light they sought to walk.

The happy, sometimes playful, intercourse between them may perhaps best be exemplified by the petition sent up by Mr. Keble on an alarm that the copse on Ladwell hill was about to be cut down in obedience to the dicta of agricultural judges who much objected to trees and broad hedgerows.

Ladwell, or as it probably ought to be, Ladywell hill, is a steep bank, thickly clothed with trees and copsewood, with cottages nestling under it, on the southward road from Hursley, and on the top the pathway to Field House, the farm rented by Dr. Moberly, Headmaster of Winchester College (since Bishop of Salisbury) as the holiday resort of his family. It is a delightful place, well worthy of the plea for its preservation.

TO THE LORD OF THE MANOR OF MERDON.

THE PETITION OF SUNDRY LIFE-TENANTS OR HEREDITARY DENIZENS OF THE SAID MANOR.

Humbly Sheweth, -

That by custom of this clime,

Even from immemorial time,

We, or our forefathers old

(As in Withering's list enrolled)

Have in occupation been

Of all nooks and corners green

Where the swelling meadows sweet

With the waving woodlands meet.

There we peep and disappear,
There, in games to fairies dear
All the spring-tide hours we spend,
Hiding, seeking without end.
And sometimes a merry train
Comes upon us from the lane:
Every gleaming afternoon
All through April, May, and June,
Boys and maidens, birds and bees,
Airy whisperings of all trees,
With their music will supply
All we need of sympathy.
Now and then a graver guest
For one moment here will rest
Loitering in his pastoral walk,
And with us hold kindly talk.
To himself we've heard him say,
"Thanks that I may hither stray,
Worn with age and sin and care,
Here to breathe the pure, glad air,
Here Faith's lesson learn anew,
Of this happy vernal crew.
Here the fragrant shrubs around,
And the graceful shadowy ground,
And the village tones afar,
And the steeple with its star,
And the clouds that gently move,
Turn the heart to trust and love."
  Thus we fared in ages past,
But the nineteenth age at last,
(As your suppliants are advised)
Reigns, and we no more are prized.

Now a giant plump and tall,
Called High Farming stalks o'er all,
Platforms, railings and straight lines,
Are the charms for which he pines.
Forms mysterious, ancient hues,
He with untired hate pursues;
And his cruel word and will
Is, from every copse-crowned hill
Every glade in meadow deep,
Us and our green bowers to sweep.
Now our prayer is, Here and there
May your Honour deign to spare
Shady spots and nooks, where we
Yet may flourish, safe and free.
So old Hampshire still may own
(Charm to other shires unknown)
Bays and creeks of grassy lawn
Half beneath his woods withdrawn;
So from many a joyous child,
Many a sire and mother mild,
For the sheltering boughs so sweet
And the blossoms at their feet,
Thanks with prayers shall find their way;
And we flowers, if we may pray,
With our very best would own
Your young floweret newly blown.
ANEMONE NEMOROSA
PRIMULA VULGARIS
ORCHIS
DAFFODIL
COWSLIP
STRAWBERRY

VIOLET

[Innumerable Signatures.] etc. etc. etc.

LADWELL HILL,

2nd April 1855.

"The young flow'ret newly blown" was Sir William's son Godfrey, who faded at seven years old. When his mind was wandering, one of his dreamy utterances was, "I should like to fly softly." And therefore Mr. Keble suggested that the words on his little grave (outside the mausoleum) should be "Who are these that fly as a cloud?"

The intercourse of the vicarage with the Park, as with all this neighbourhood, was affectionate, intimate, or neighbourly and friendly, according as there was likeness of mind. The impression left was always a cheerful one of hospitality and of a kind of being on holy ground. The house stands on the side of a rapid slope from the Park, with a terrace raised on brick arches overlooking the lawn, only separated by a low wall from the Churchyard. Here, in early summer, the school children from both the outlying congregations met those of Hursley at tea, and for games in the Park, ending with standing round in the twilight below the terrace, and singing the National Anthem and Bishop Ken's Evening Hymn. The Anniversary of the Consecration Day, falling late in the autumn, was the occasion of a feast for the elders of the parish above sixty years old. This followed, of course, on festal services, when those who heard it can hardly forget a sermon of Warden Barter's on the 134th Psalm, when, with the noble sweetness of his countenance lighted up, he spoke of our delight in nature being the joy of a child in the beauty of his father's house.

A new organ had been given, and the choir had been brought to great improvement during the few years that the Rev. W. Le Geyt was at Hursley. Also a mission school chapel had been built at Pitt, a hamlet on the downs towards Winchester, and a second curate had been added to the staff. The present writer can only dwell with thankfulness too deep to be spoken on Mr. Keble's influence, not so much friendly as fatherly, and he was the best and kindest of critics in literary affairs.

But throughout, the vicar was the personal minister to each individual of his flock - teaching in the school, catechising in the church, most carefully preparing for Confirmation, watching over the homes, and, however otherwise busied, always at the beck and call of every one in the parish. To the old men and women of the workhouse he paid special attention, bringing them little dainties, trying to brighten their dull minds as a means of reaching their souls, and endeavouring to raise their spirits to higher things. One who had been removed to another Union, when asked how he liked Hursley, said, "It seemed as if they was saying Holy, Holy, Holy, all day long."

During this time Mr. Keble wrote his Life of Bishop Wilson, making two visits to the Isle of Man to study the situation and the documents there preserved; various of the "Plain Sermons"; some controversial pamphlets defending the cause of the Church; and above all, the treatise on "Eucharistic Adoration." He assisted Dr. J. M. Neale in drawing up the Salisbury Hymnal, a precursor of Hymns Ancient and Modern, and contributed several hymns, especially those for Rogation days, for the service for Holy Matrimony, and a very grand one for the Feast of St. John the Evangelist, which has not found place in Hymns Ancient and Modern.

All this time he was the prime counsellor and assistant to many engaged in church work or church defence, among whom may be mentioned Dr. Pusey, Bishop Alexander Forbes of Brechin, Bishop Walter Hamilton of Salisbury, the Rev. W. J. Butler of Wantage (Dean of Lincoln), and Canon Liddon. To them Hursley Vicarage was a place of holy counsel and peaceful rest.

Bishop Robert Gray of Capetown, and the great Bishop George Augustus Selwyn, were warmly welcomed there on their visits to England; and the young son of the last-mentioned, John Richardson Selwyn, when left in England for education, often happily spent part of his holidays there. No doubt this had a share in his preparation for his future work in Melanesia, closed early by the failure of health that brought him, after a few more years, to his grave.

Another guest was Queen Emma of the Sandwich Isles, literally the Queen of the South, come to hear the wisdom of the Saint; and last of all, the friend and partner of his earlier work, the sharer in the revival of the Church from her torpid repose, John Henry Newman, who met Dr. Pusey there for one last day, fulfilling the words written long before -

Yet deem not on such parting sad

Shall dawn no welcome dear and glad.

But neither of these two last visits took place till after the changes of old age had begun at Hursley.

The first great sorrow came in the death of Elisabeth, the wise, gentle, and quiet invalid sister who had been always part of Mr. Keble's life, and seemed, above all, to diffuse about her an atmosphere of peace and holiness. After a gradual, almost imperceptible decay, she sank to sleep on the 7th of August 1860. Mrs. Keble's always frail health began to fail more and more, so that winters in a warmer climate became necessary. Dawlish, Penzance, and Torquay were resorted to in successive winters, and Mr. Keble began to revolve the question whether it might not become his duty to resign the living, where, to his own humble apprehension, all his best efforts had failed to raise the people to his own standard of religion. However, this was averted, and he was still at his post when, on the night of St. Andrew's Day, the 30th of November 1864, as he was sitting up writing to Dean Stanley on a passage of which he disapproved in the History of the Jewish Church, the hand of warning touched him with a slight stroke of paralysis. With complete rest at Torquay and Penzance during the winter, he recovered to a considerable degree, and came home to resume many of his usual habits, but Mrs. Keble's suffering from spasmodic asthma had become very frequent, and it became necessary, early in the autumn, to remove to Bournemouth.

There they remained, she gradually sinking, and only distressed at the thought of his being left; he bearing up in silent resignation and prayer till, on the 22nd of March, a mistake in using a cold instead of a hot bath brought on a shock, and in four days more, on Maundy-Thursday the 29th of March 1866, the voice of Hursley and Otterbourne was, "Thy master is taken from thy head to-day." It was granted to her to be at rest concerning him before she followed, six weeks later, on the 11th of May, to the double grave.

It was on a beautiful day, with the celandines shining like stars on the bank, that we laid him in his grave, a concourse of sorrowing friends being present, who could look to him as having wakened and cherished their best aspirations; and those who had come under his personal influence feeling that a loved father had been taken away. It was on that day that Alexander Forbes, Bishop of Brechin, Dr. Pusey, Dean Hook, Sir William Heathcote, Dean Butler, and others, decided that the most fitting memorial would be the building of the College at Oxford which bears his name, and is pledged to Church principles, and to a scale of expenses not beyond the reach of less wealthy students. A monument was in due time raised above the graves, designed by Mr. Butterfield - Mr. Keble's in red granite, Mrs. Keble's in Derbyshire marble.

CHAPTER XIII - LATER CHANGES

In the October of 1853, the Rev. Robert F. Wilson having resigned the curacy of Ampfield, he was replaced by the Rev. John Frewen Moor, who on 12th January of the next year became perpetual curate and by and by vicar.

Improvements in the church advanced in his time. The stained glass of the east and west windows of the church were given by Sir William and Lady Heathcote, the south-east window is a memorial of Mr. Keble, the other south windows of Mr. Moor's three sons, one of whom was drowned while preparing for mission work in Newfoundland, and another died on his return from what was truly a pilgrimage to the Holy Land.

On Mr. Keble's death, the Rev. James Gavin Young, brother to the much beloved curate, the Rev. Peter Young, was presented to the living of Hursley.

In 1871 the Rev. William Bigg Wither, after thirty-five years' diligent work in the parish, decided on accepting the rectory of Hardwicke in Buckinghamshire. Great improvements had taken place in his time, and he was greatly beloved by his flock, from whom, for nearly forty years, he had never been absent for a single Sunday, and during all that time had given them the privilege of daily matins and evensong.

As he never liked the acceptance of testimonials, it was resolved that, in memory of his long services, a new girls' school should be built, the old one having become quite insufficient, and with it a master's house with a tower to contain a village clock, which was given out of the savings of Mrs. Smith and her sister and brother Miss and Mr. Pink, a kind old thatcher, who will long be remembered.

In that year, 1869, Bishop Sumner resigned the see of Winchester, and for three years the diocese had the benefit of the great powers and eloquence of Bishop Samuel Wilberforce, whose Confirmation addresses at each of the churches will be remembered for life by his candidates.

The Rev. Walter Francis Elgie became Mr. Young's curate at Otterbourne, and in 1875 the first vicar thereof, Sir William Heathcote having arranged the means of undoing Bishop Pontissara's injustice. This was rendered practicable by the liberality of Mrs. William Gibbs, who purchased the advowson of Otterbourne for a sum that Sir William applied to the endowment of Hursley, so as to compensate for the loss of the tithes of Otterbourne.

By this time a considerable industry had grown up at Allbrook with a saw mill and brick making, and the inhabitants, with a little assistance, erected a mission chapel and school. There the kind and excellent Rowland Jones Bateman, Esquire, of the Grange, gave hearty assistance as a teacher, and latterly as a licensed reader, being thus appointed by Bishop Edward Harold Browne, who succeeded to the See of Winchester on the sudden death of Bishop Wilberforce.

He came to reconsecrate Otterbourne Church, when an apse had been added to the choir, and several other alterations made, with the view of rendering it more suitable for devout worship than knowledge or means had made practicable when the church was built; and other alterations have since been made in the same direction.

The kindly and open-hearted Squire of Cranbury, Thomas Chamberlayne, Esq., died on October 1876, being succeeded by his son Tankerville Chamberlayne, Esq.; and Brambridge, after descending from the Smythes to a niece, the Honourable Mrs. Craven, whose son sold it, has since several times changed owners.

On the 25th February 1881, Otterbourne lost the first vicar, Mr. Elgie, and the Rev. Henry Walter Brock was presented to the vicarage, when many improvements were further carried on.

But change and decay mark every generation in turn, and there is little else to record. The joyous genial days at Hursley Park had passed away, and the days of agricultural depression had set in, causing much trouble and anxiety, with alterations met with simple bravery and cheerfulness, according with the character that could bear adversity as nobly as prosperity.

The Rev. Thomas Mozley, in the somewhat discursive reminiscences of his latter years, declares that long before, he had seen one of Mr. Keble's curates in tears at the possibility of the repeal of the Corn-Laws causing Sir William Heathcote to put down one of his equipages. None of the curates could recollect the occasion, and certainly they lived to see what might have been more deplored, for at the end of Sir William's life there were actually only two little ponies in his stables.

Though never a very strong man, he preserved all his powers and his kind interest and thorough attention to whatever was brought before him until the end came, as to "a shock of corn in full season," and he was taken to his rest on the 17th of August 1881, leaving to all who knew him the precious recollection of emphatically "a just man" serving God in his generation.

That simple walking funeral, devoid of all pomp or show, but attended by at least 130 friends, did indeed show the esteem in which he was held as the moving spring of all the best undertakings for many years in the county; and may Hursley never forget that she is, as it were, consecrated by having been the home of two such men as John Keble and William Heathcote.

Still there are changes to record: Julian Bargus Yonge, after long inactivity from broken health, sold the property at Otterbourne to Major Robert Scarlett, and removed to London, where he died a few days later, in October 1891.

In 1892 Mr. Brock was invited to return to his house in Guernsey to become rector of the parish of St. Pierre au Bois in succession to his father and grandfather, and the Rev. Henry Albany Bowles became vicar of Otterbourne.

Other changes had in the meantime taken place. The Hursley estate, including not only the Manor of Merdon but recent purchases, had become much encumbered from the inevitable consequences of agricultural depression, and after the provision for the family had been made, of whom there were ten survivors besides Lady Heathcote, it proved that the only way of clearing off the various liabilities was to sell.

Lady Heathcote gave up her right to a life residence at Hursley Park, and after 170 years of possession, during which the family had well merited general affection and esteem, they resigned themselves to the sale of the greater part of the property. The Park, the advowson of the living, and the greater part of the parish, were bought by Joseph Baxendale, Esq., in 1888.

The more distant portions were more gradually disposed of, and recently the ground of Cranbury Common and Hiltingbury has risen in value from brick-making industries, and the convenience of Chandler's (or Chaloner's) Ford Station, and a large and rising colony, on the confines of five parishes, Otterbourne, North Stoneham, Ampfield, Hursley, and Baddesley. A school chapel was raised, but soon proved insufficient, and there is now a church. The place has been formed into a separate parish, Otterbourne resigning the hamlet of Fryern Hill; Ampfield, part of Fryern Hill and numerous houses built among the plantations of Cuckoo Bushes and Cranbury Common; and Stoneham, many houses placed among the trees of the former Fleming property.

And another change took place, Mr. Frewen Moor, from increasing age and loss of eyesight, resigned the pastoral charge he had so carefully and affectionately fulfilled for forty-four years, and was succeeded by the Rev. Vere Awdry.

RECTORS AND VICARS OF HURSLEY.

John de Raleghe, Rector d. 1279

Paganus de Lyskeret, Rector 1280-1296

   John de Sta. Fide, Vicar

Hugo de Welewyck, Rector 1296-1348

   Henry de Lyskeret, Vicar

   Roger de la Vere, Vicar

William de Ffarlee, Vicar 1348-1363

William de Middleton, Vicar 1363-1392

John Cove, Vicar 1392-1412

Walter Cowper Vicar 1412.

John Langshaw, Vicar before 1447-1454

William Emery, Vicar 1454

John Lovyer, Vicar 1482

William Capell, Vicar about 1529

John Hynton, Vicar deprived 1565

Richard Foxe, Vicar 1565

William Symmons, Vicar 1581-1616

John Cole, Vicar 1616-1638
John Hardy, Vicar 1638 ejected 1645
(Several Puritan Intruders.)
Robert Maunder, 1660-1673
Thomas Pretty, 1673-1684
Matthew Leadbeater, 1684-1707
Edward Griffiths, 1707-1726
Richard Newcome, 1726-1747
William White, 1747-1780
Samuel Gauntlett, 1780-1804
Gilbert Heathcote, 1804-1829
Gilbert Wall Heathcote, 1829-1835
John Keble, 1836-1866
James Gavin Young, 1866

CHAPTER XIV - A SURVEY

It may be best to conclude with a sketch of the present appearance of the parishes (in 1898).

To begin at the west, where the border is on Romsey, Michelmersh and Farley, the Romsey road, formerly the direct road from Winchester to Salisbury, running through it, beside Ampfield Church and village. This is high ground, and Ampfield Wood extends along it to the borders of Hursley Park. It is chiefly of oak, fir, and beech, and on the southern side are the fine arcades of beechwood that Mr. Keble used to call Hursley Cathedral. From one point in the wood long sight can distinguish a sort of needle which is the spire of Salisbury Cathedral. The wood is very old, probably primeval, as it is guarded in the oldest notices of the Manor of Merdon, and it contains a flora of its own, in which may be mentioned that rare and beautiful Melittis Melissophyllum, bastard balm, like a purple and white archangel. The bilberry is plentiful there and all along the beautiful park-like road to Romsey and Salisbury. The church, raised above the wayside fountain, and the churchyard full of very beautiful varieties of pine, still nestles into the wood, and there is a charming view over the open country towards the south.

Farley Chamberlayne, which joins the wood on the other side, rising much higher, has a monument viewed from all the country round, erected by one of the St. John family to a horse which leapt down with him into a chalk-pit of considerable depth, and so alighted that neither horse nor man was hurt, and the horse won the cup at the races the year after, under the name of Beware Chalk-Pit. Parnholt wood, that clothes one side of the mount, is beloved by botanists for possessing tracts of lily of the valley, Convallaria majalis, and likewise Paris quadrifolia, a great rarity. The mount itself is bare chalk down, but has a wonderful view over the whole undulating country - to the southward the beginning of forest land, and to the south-east, where the beechwoods of South Lynch begin to creep up the rapid slope of chalk, there is delightful hunting ground; for bee orchis (Ophrys apifera) swarm; careful search may discover the brown velvet blue-eyed fly, Ophrys muscifera, the quaint man and dwarf orchis can be found; butterfly or honey-suckle orchis, Habenaria, as we are constrained to term it, is frequent; and where the beech-trees begin there are those curious parasites which are the only plants they tolerate, the Listera Nidus-avis, birds'-nest orchis, the Monotropa Hypopitys, or yellow birds'-nest, the beautiful lily-like Epipactis Grandiflora; while helleborine and the curious and capricious tooth-wort, Spiræa Filipendula or drop-wort, Gentiana Amarella, and other distinctive chalk-down plants are found.

On the southern side of Ampfield lies the parish of North Baddesley, which preserves the curious old Hampshire village church with a timber bell turret. This side is where there once stood a Gospel oak, marking the place where the Gospel was read, when the bounds of the Manor of Merdon were   trod   at Rogation-tide. The whole tract is an extension of the New Forest land, almost all heather and bog, undulating and, in the drier spots, growing bushes of the glistening holly. It is forest scenery without the trees, excepting the plantations of fir made by a former generation, but presenting grand golden fields of gorse in the spring, and of red and purple heather in early autumn; and whereas the northern side of Hursley gives the distinctive flora of dry chalk, here we have the growth of the black peaty bog, the great broom-rape, brown and leafless, growing on the roots of the gorse; the curious dodder spreading a tangled red skein of thread over it gemmed with little round white balls, the rare marsh cinquefoil, the brilliant yellow asphodel, the delicate, exquisite, bog pimpernel, the blue skull-cap, the two weird and curious sun-dews, and even in former times the beautiful dark blue Gentiana Pneumonanthe, as well as the two pinguiculas - Vulgaris, like a violet, and the rarer Lusitanica.

But alas! the giant called "High Farming" is an enemy to the botanists, and had starved out many of the choicest of these, even before the building of villas at Chandler's Ford put a total end to most of them.

Hursley Park touches on one side the forest land of Ampfield Wood, and on the other the chalk of the South Downs, and it shows its length of having been reclaimed in the well-kept trees with their straight lines finishing their foliage beneath, due to the feeding of deer and cattle. Its chief beauty is when the thorns are like masses of snow. Moreover, there grows up from the moat at Merdon, over the back of the remains of the gateway, a traveller's joy with an enormous trunk that must be of many years' duration. Merdon Castle is just where the chalk begins, and from thence, running down to the house itself, there is a broad level space of deer park clear of trees, and making a fit setting to the early Georgian red brick house with the gardens on the other side, containing several fine old lime-trees. On all the sides, except towards Ampfield, the ground falls away, and the village of well-kept, picturesque cottages lies in the valley beneath the park, the tall white spire of the church making a beautiful object looking along the walnut avenue leading from the gardens.

The lime-trees enclose the church on three sides most fitly, except in the eyes of an old woman, some sixty years ago, who objected to worshipping in a grove.

At a short distance eastward of the churchyard begin the two roads, both leading to Otterbourne; the northern one, part of which still bears the name of King's Lane, is said to have been the way taken by Purkis's cart when bringing William Rufus's body to Winchester.

The southern road, which is part of the Romsey and Southampton highway, soon rises into the height of Ladwell Hill, fields with very fine elms bordering it on the west, and the copse of Mr. Keble's petition on the east. At the gate of the wood is a patch of the rare Geranium Phæun, the dusky crane's-bill, but whether wild, or a stray from a disused garden, is doubtful.

After another dip, the road to Otterbourne leaves the main one, and skirts Cranbury Park, and has on the opposite side the once open country, since planted first with trees and later with houses, leading to Chandler's Ford. The very pretty and uncommon Linaria repens, a toad flax, white and striped with purple, is a speciality that it is hoped may not be smothered with houses and gardens. A lane, called even in 1588 Mallibar, runs southward over the heath, and emerges into the Southampton road. It is a grand place for heath, ferns, and broom-rape, with daffodils in a field at the end. There are remains of a farm-yard and orchard, once apparently rented by Mr. Coram of Cranbury.

Cranbury Park is on a hill, intersected by various springs, and where the peaty ground soon gives way to gravel. The house, a large red brick one, built round a court, so that it looks low in proportion to its width, is on the level ground at the top, flat as it fronts to the south, but in the rear descending rapidly. In fact, on that side the grounds have the air of cresting the hill, and there is a group of exceedingly tall pine-trees which are a land-mark of the country on all sides, though the tallest of them was blown down a few years ago. Near them is one of the old-fashioned orangeries, with a great deal of wall and very little glass, and near it stands the sundial of Newtonian fame.

From the ridge where the pines stand the ground descends through very steep fields belonging to the Home Farm at Longmore to King's Lane, where Hursley parish touches upon Compton, at the hamlet of Silkstede, which is reported to have been a priory, and has a fine old barn and a dell in the orchard full of snowdrops. No mention of it is in Dugdale's Monasticon, and it was probably only a grange; but it still owns some very fine old trees, the bordering copses are full of violets, and the rare Lathyrus Nissolia has been found there.

Returning to the open park in front of Cranbury, there occurs that fitfully blooming plant, lady's-tresses - Neottia Spiralis autumnalis - and a profusion of brown-winged orchis and cowslips. All the slopes are covered with copsewood, much of it oak, the tints of which are lovely shades of green in spring and golden-brown in early autumn. The whole is a place remarkable for masses of blossom. There are giant garlands of white wild cherry above in spring, and equally white anemone below; by and by an acre of primroses growing close together, not large, but wonderfully thick, a golden river of king-cup between banks of dog's mercury, later on whole glades of wild hyacinth, producing a curious effect of blue beneath the budding yellow green of the young birches with silver stems. Sheets of the scarlet sorrel by and by appear, and foxgloves of all sizes troop in the woods, and are succeeded by the rose bay willow herb, and lastly come perfect clouds of the little devils'-bit scabious. Ferns adorn the watery glens, and bracken spreads on the undulating ground in wild beauty of form, here and there enhanced by a bright faded tint of gold.

At the bottom of the hill, close to Otterbourne Church, the gravel has given place to clay. On the side of the hill, a rough hedge divides the private ground of the copse from Otterbourne Common and Hill, which is crossed by the old high road from London to Southampton, the very steep hill having had a cutting made through it. The Cranbury side of the road has the village cricket ground on it, though burrowed under by the concentric brick-work circles of the Southampton Company's water works, which are entered by a little staircase tower, cemented over so as to be rather ornamental than otherwise. Beside it, there is a beautiful view of a delightful home landscape; stretching out on the south lie woods and low hills to the gleam of Southampton Water, the smoke of the steamers, and even the gray hills of the Isle of Wight. On the other side, beyond the rich water meadows of the Itchen valley, may be seen the woods of Colden Common rising into Concord Hill, and beyond them the view is closed by the broken outline of Longwood Warren. While more to the north there is visible the round smooth outline of "the beech-crowned steep" of St. Catherine's Hill. It is a charming prospect, especially on a day of sunshine and clouds, making shadows chase one another over the distance. Nor, except for a white thatched cottage and an extensive gravel-pit by the road, have the native charms of the hill been much disturbed; and gorse, heather, and honeysuckle flourish till, where the clay begins, there is a grassy slope bearing a few elms and horse-chestnuts. Perhaps loaded waggons drop some of their seeds, for on those cuttings through the gravel on the road-side have sprung up the dainty little yellow stonecrop, Sedum acre, and the Stork's bill, Erodium moschatum. These are plentifully spread over the cutting; but theTrifolium arvense, which came for a few years, seems to have vanished again.

On the eastern side of the road lies the village green. The old cottages used to stand round in an irregular amphitheatre, some with poplars before them, and the name of Maypole-field (now allotments) testifies to there having been sports there before the memory of the present man. The arrangements have been broken by modern building, but "right of common" still protects the green expanse for donkeys and children, including the more youthful cricketers, not yet promoted to matches.

From the top of the hill extends a large space of woodland known as Otterbourne Park. The higher part is full of a growth of beautiful ling, in delicate purple spikes, almost as tall as the hazel and mountain ash are allowed to grow. On summer evenings it is a place in which to hear the nightingale, and later to see the glow-worm, and listen to the purring of the nightjar. It is a very ancient wood, part of the original grant of St. Magdalen College, and bears plenty of the yellow cow-wheat which Kingsley holds as the mark of primeval waste-land; but it is not exceptional in its other plants, except that a spring, half-way down, has the rare Viola palustris around it. The whole tract remained untouched till a pleasant residence called the Grange was taken out of it to the south, at a ground rent, by Rowland Jones Bateman, Esq., whose beneficent kindness and excellent religious influence told on all the neighbourhood, and especially on the hamlet of Allbrook, till his death in 1897.

The parish here borders on Bishopstoke, and the Grange commands a pleasant view over the water meadows, and up the opposite Bishopstoke Hill. Otterbourne Park reaches down to where the meadows begin along the course of the Itchen.

In these meadows, the will-of-the-wisp has undoubtedly been seen, as well as in a wet field in the central part of the parish; but it is a disappointing phenomenon - nothing but a misty, pale bluish light, rather like the reality of a comet's tail, and if "he" was by "Friar's Lantern led," "he" must have had a strong imagination.

Probably drainage, sawmills, and brick-making have exorcised Jack-o'-Lantern, for Allbrook, from a hamlet of four cottages, has grown up into a considerable village, with a school-chapel of its own, and a large population. The two farms called Hams and Boyatt border it on the southern or Bishopstoke side, and on the northern it extends to Highbridge (apparently so called from the lowness of the bridge), where is another small hamlet, half Otterbourne half Twyford; and there was for many years a Roman Catholic chapel attached to a large cottage, and distinguished by a cross. It was endowed, but nearly all the flock having faded away, the endowment was transferred to Eastleigh, and it is now inhabited by a market gardener with numerous glass houses.

It is the real Itchen that is crossed at Highbridge. The canal goes through Allbrook, but both serve the purpose of irrigation, and a network of ditches crosses the meadows. Both river and canal, too, are excellent for fishermen, who in the season can find

here and there a lusty trout,

And here and there a grayling

in the clear stream, which now and then an otter inhabits, soon to serve as sport for his many enemies.

Smooth and level, the river is still an unfailing source of enjoyment in the walks along the towing path, when moor-hens are swimming, and dipping on a glimpse of the spectator; when fish are rising, or sometimes taking a sudden "header" into the air and going down with a splash; when the water-vole rushes for his hole with head just above the water; when a blue flash of kingfisher darts by, and the deep blue or green dragon-flies sit on the sedges, or perhaps a tiny May-fly sits on a rail to shake off its last garment, and come forth a snow-white fairy thing with three long whisks at the tail.

The real Itchen is the boundary, and beyond lies Brambridge. But on coming to the bridge over the canal, the road leads westward, towards Otterbourne Hill. First it skirts a stream, a tributary to the Itchen, and goes between meadows till the old church is reached, now only a chancel in the midst of old headstones, and still bordered with trees on the bank between it and the stream. There are square brick monuments covered with stone slabs. In the interstices there used to be a great deal of Adiantum nigrum - black maidenhair, but it has disappeared.

The flowers are quite different from those of the peaty marshes on the opposite side of the district, belonging to an alluvial soil, washed down from the chalk hills. The great reed-mace adorns the Itchen, and going along the disused towing path of the canal there is to be found abundance of the black and golden spikes of the sedge, and the curious balls of the bur-reed, very like the horrid German weapon called a morning star. Also meadow-sweet, meadow-rue, and comfrey of every shade of purple, the water avens and forget-me-not, also that loveliest plant the bog-bean, with trefoil leaves and feathery blossoms. Orchis latifolia is in plenty, and also Orchis incarnata, sometimes called the Romsey orchis. Of late years the mimulus has gilded the bank of one of the ditches. Is it compensation for the Pinguicula vulgaris, which has been drained away, or the mountain pink at Highbridge, which I suspect some gardener of appropriating? Higher up the course of the river, Orchis conopsea, long-spurred and very sweet, the compact Orchis pyramidalis, and the rare Epipactis palustris are to be found, as well as Campanula Glomerata, and crow garlic, in an old chalk-pit nearly destroyed by the railway and the water works.

Otterbourne Farm bounds the churchyard on the west side, and below, on either side of a low bridge, stand two fine yew trees where boys in the old church days used to climb and devour the waxen berries with impunity. Meadows lie on each side the road, and on the left is a short lane, leading up to the old manor house, the Moat-house but it is no longer even a farm-house - the moat is choked with mud and reeds, and only grows fine forget-me-nots, and the curious panel picture of a battle, apparently between Turks and Austrians, has been removed. The fields beyond, bordering on Otterbourne Park, are the best for cowslips in the parish.

Returning into the road, whose proper name is Kiln Lane, the way leads between two fields, oddly enough called Courtiers, rising a little, and with a view of Otterbourne Hill, the east side of which, below the slope of Otterbourne Park, has been laid out in allotments for more than fifty years, at first by Mr. Yonge, though it has now been taken in hand by the Parish Council, and it makes a pleasant picture of stripes of various shades of green and brown with people working in them. The hedge sweeps round in a curve, leaving a space where stands the Pound, still sometimes used for straying cattle. The Stocks were once there, but never used in the memory of man.

The valley is of clay, strong yellow clay favourable to oaks, though too many have been cut down, whenever they came to a good size in the hedges; but in the grounds of Otterbourne House, where they have been undisturbed for at least eighty years, there are a number of very handsome well-grown trees; and near them is Dell Copse, dug out for the bricks for the "King's House," and the home of countless daffodils. Half way up the hill is a small spring, where the water rises so as to make little jets of sand. It flows down in a gutter to the green at the opening of Kiln Lane, around the Pound, and here spreads into a pool, called the Dip Hole, the resort of cows from the common, and long of village women, as the blue galt below the yellow clay never affords good water, but this has been remedied by water works.

At this spot Kiln Lane opens into the high-road, and there is a broad space of green at nearly the bottom of the hill, before the main body of the village begins. Every line in the place is a curve-hedges, roads, gardens and all, and this gives the view a peculiar grace, so that one of the old men used to say he knew not where to find a better or prettier view than looking down into the village from the hill, and on far beyond to Owslebury, Crowd Hill, and Longwood Warren, a lovely home view.

The church stands on the hillside just where the upward road to Cranbury begins to branch off. The churchyard is full of crosses, a large granite cross in memory of John Keble as rector in the midst, and there is a splendid Wellingtonia, or more properly a Sequoia, now about fifty years old, and overtopping the bell-turret. And the outside space on this side is scattered with horse chestnuts and elms.

Below are the schools, and the irregular curving street of houses, thatched, tiled, or slated, in gardens or close to the road. Here stands Otterbourne House, and, after two large fields, more cottages, and the vicarage, like the schools, with the fancy brick chimneys moulded at Hursley.

Not far beyond, the little stream that had crossed the meadows from the church is spanned by another bridge, belonging to the high-road from Winchester. Thence may be seen the source of the stream, in Pool Hole, said to be fed from Merdon well, and now forced to spread into a bed of watercresses.

And here begins Compton, Silkstede is in sight, and the round of the parishes is completed with King's Lane, turning to the west from the high road to Winchester.

CHAPTER XV - WORDS AND PHRASES

Before entirely quitting the parish, a few of the older words and forms of expression may be recorded, chiefly as remembered from the older generation, for "the schoolmaster" and the influx of new inhabitants have changed much that was characteristic of the genuine West Saxon. Nor, indeed, was there any very pronounced dialect, like a separate language. The speech is slow, and with a tendency to make o like aa, as Titus Oates does in Peveril of the Peak. An Otterbourne man going into Devonshire was told, "My son, you speak French." No one ever showed the true Hampshire south-country speech and turn of expression so well as Lady Verney in her Lettice Lisle, and she has truly Hampshire characters too, such as could once easily be matched in these villages.

The words and phrases here set down are only what can be vouched for by those who have grown up to them

WORDS

Caddle, untidy condition.

"In he comes when I'm all of a caddle."

To stabble, to walk about aimlessly, or in the wet.

"Now, Miss, don't you come stabbling in and out when I am scouring."

Or,

"I can't come stabbling down that there dirty lane, or I should be all of a muck."

Want, mole.

Chiselbob, woodlouse; also called a cud-worm, and, rolled in a pill, put down the throat of a cow to promote the restoration of her cud, which she was supposed to have lost.

Gowk, cuckoo.

Fuzz-Buzz, traveller's joy.

Palmer, caterpillar.

Dish-washer, water-wagtail.

Chink, chaffinch.

Long-tailed caper, long-tailed tit.

Yaffil, green woodpecker.

"The yaffil laughed loud." - See Peacock at Home.

Smellfox, anemone.

Dead men's fingers, orchis.

Granny's night-cap, water avens.

Jacob's ladder, Solomon's seal.

Lady's slipper, Prunella vulgaris.

Poppy, foxglove.

To routle, to rummage (like a pig in straw).

To terrify, to worry or disturb.

"Poor old man, the children did terrify him so, he is gone into the Union."

Wind-list, white streak of faint cloud across a blue sky, showing the direction of the wind.

Shuffler, man employed about a farmyard.

Randy go, uproar.

"I could not sleep for that there randy go they was making."

Pook, a haycock.

All of a pummy, all of a moulter, because it was so very brow, describing the condition of a tree, which shattered as it fell because it was brow, i.e. brittle.

Leer, empty, generally said of hunger. - See German.

Hulls, chaff. The chaff of oats; used to be in favour for stuffing mattresses.

Heft, Weight.

To huck, to push or pull out. Scotch (howk).

Stook, the foundation of a bee hive.

Pe-art, bright, lively, the original word bearht for both bright and pert.

Loo (or lee), sheltered.

Steady, slow.

"She is so steady I can't do nothing with her."

Kickety, said of a one-sided wheel-barrow that kicked up (but this may have been invented for the nonce).

Pecty, covered with little spots of decay.

Fecty, defective throughout - both used in describing apples or potatoes.

Hedge-picks, shoes.

Hags or aggarts, haws.

Rauch, smoke (comp. German and Scotch).

Pond-keeper, dragon-fly.

Stupid, ill-conditioned.

To plim, to swell, as bacon boiled.

To side up, to put tidy.

Logie, poorly, out-of-sorts.

VILLAGE SPECIFICS.

Cure for Epilepsy

To wear round the neck a bag with a hair from the cross on a he-donkey.

Or,

To wear a ring made of sixpences begged from six young women who married without change of name.

Cure for Whooping Cough

An infusion of mouse ear hawkweed (Hieracium Pilosella), flavoured with thyme and honey. This is really effective, like other "yarbs" that used to be in vogue.

Cure for Shingles

Grease off church bells.

For Sore Throat

Rasher of fat bacon fastened round the neck.

For Ague

To be taken to the top of a steep place, then violently pushed down.

Or,

To have gunpowder in bags round the wrists set on fire.

Powdered chaney (china), a general specific.

PHRASES

Singing psalms to a dead horse, exhorting a stolid subject.

Surplice, smock-frock.

"Ah! sir, the white surplice covers a great deal of dirt" - said by a tidy woman of her old father.

"And what be I to pay you?"

"What the Irishman shot at," i.e. nothing - conversation overheard between an old labourer and his old friend, the thatcher, who had been mending his roof.

"Well, dame, how d'ye fight it out?" - salutation overheard.

CURATE. Have you heard the nightingale yet?

BOY. Please, sir, I don't know how he hollers.

Everything hollers, from a church bell to a mouse in a trap.

A tenth child, if all the former ones are living, is baptized with a sprig of myrtle in his cap, and the clergyman was supposed to charge himself with his education.

If possible, a baby was short-coated on Good Friday, to ensure not catching cold.

The old custom (now gone out) was that farmers should send their men to church on Good Friday. They used all to appear in their rough dirty smock frocks and go back to work again. Some (of whom it would never have been expected) would fast all day.

The 29th of May is still called Shick-shack day - why has never been discovered. There must have been some observance earlier than the Restoration, though oak-apples are still worn on that day, and with their oak sprays are called Shick-shack.

On St. Clement's Day, the 23rd of November, explosions of gunpowder are made on country blacksmiths' anvils. It is viewed as the blacksmiths' holiday. The accepted legend is that St. Clement was drowned with an anchor hung to his neck, and that his body was found in a submarine temple, from which the sea receded every seven years for the benefit of pilgrims. Thus he became the patron of anchor forgers, and thence of smiths in general. Charles Dickens, in Great Expectations describes an Essex blacksmith as working to a chant, the refrain of which was "Old Clem." I have heard the explosions at Hursley before 1860, but more modern blacksmiths despise the custom. At Twyford, however, the festival is kept, and at the dinner a story is read that after the Temple was finished, Solomon feasted all the artificers except the blacksmiths, but they appeared, and pointed out all that they had done in the way of necessary work, on which they were included with high honour.

St. Thomas's Day, 21st December, is still at Otterbourne held as the day for "gooding," when each poor house-mother can demand sixpence from the well-to-do towards her Christmas dinner.

Christmas mummers still perambulate the villages, somewhat uncertainly, as their performance depends on the lads willing to undertake it, and the willingness of some woman to undertake the bedizening of them with strips of ribbon or coloured paper; and, moreover, political allusions are sometimes introduced which spoil the simplicity. The helmets are generally made of wallpaper, in a shape like auto-da-fé caps, with long strips hanging over so as to conceal the face, and over the shirts are sewn streamers.

Thus tramp seven or eight lads, and stand drawn up in a row, when the foremost advances with, at the top of his hoarse voice:

Room, room, brave gallants, room,

I'm just come to show you some merry sport and game,

To help pass away

This cold winter day.

Old activity, new activity, such activity

As never was seen before,

And perhaps never will be seen no more.

(Alas! too probably. Thanks to the schoolmaster abroad.)

Then either he or some other, equipped with a little imitation snow, paces about announcing himself:

Here comes I, Old Father Christmas, Christmas, Christmas,

Welcome or welcome not,
I hope old Father Christmas
Will never be forgot.
All in this room, there shall be shown
The dreadfullest battle that ever was known.
So walk in, St. George, with thy free heart
And see whether thou canst claim peace for thine own part.

So far from "claiming peace," St. George waves (or ought to wave) his wooden sword, as he clumps forth, exclaiming:

In comes I, St. George, St. George, that man of courage bold,
With my broad sword and spear I won the crown of gold,
I fought that fiery dragon,
And drove him to the slaughter,
And by that means I won
The King of Egypt's daughter.
Therefore, if any man dare enter this door
I'll hack him small as dust,
And after send him to the cook's shop
To be made into mince-pie crust!

On this defiance another figure appears:

Here comes I, the Turkish knight
Just come from Turkey land to fight;
I'll fight thee, St. George, St. George, thou man of courage bold,
If thy blood be too hot, I'll quickly make it cold.

To which St. George responds, in the tone in which he would address a cart-horse:

"Wo ho! My little fellow, thou talk'st very bold,
Just like the little Turks, as I have been told,
Therefore, thou Turkish knight,
Pull out thy sword and fight,
Pull out thy purse and pay,
I'll have satisfaction, or thou guest away.

Turkish Knight.

Satisfaction, no satisfaction at all,

My head is made of iron, my body lined with steel,

I'll battle thee, to see which on the ground shall fall.

The two wooden swords clatter together till the Turkish knight falls, all doubled up, even his sword, with due regard to his finery; and St. George is so much shocked that he marches round, lamenting:

O only behold what I have been and done,

Cut and slain my brother, just the evening sun.

Then, bethinking himself, he exclaims:

I have a little bottle, called elecampane,

If the man is alive, let him rise and fight again.

The application of the elecampane so far restores the Turkish knight that he partly rises, entreating:

O pardon me, St. George, O pardon me, I crave,

O pardon me this once, and I will be thy slave.

Very inconsistently with his late remorse, St. George replies -

I never will pardon a Turkish knight,

Therefore arise, and try thy might.

The combat is renewed, and the Turkish knight falls prostrate, on which the Foreign King comes forward, shouting:

St. George, St. George, what hast thou done,

For thou hast slain mine only son!

But, after marching round the fallen hero, he cries:

Is there a doctor to be found,

That can cure this man lies bleeding on the ground?

In response, the doctor appears:

O yes, there is a doctor to be found,

That can cure this man lies bleeding on the ground.

The anxious father asks:

Doctor, doctor, what is thy fee?

The doctor replies:

Ten guineas is my fee,

But ten pounds I'll take of thee.

The king answers:

"Take it, doctor, but what canst thou cure?"

The doctor's pretensions are high, for he says:

I can cure the ague, palsy, and the gout,

And that's a roving pain that goes within and out;

A broken leg or arm, I soon can cure the pain,

And if thou break'st thy neck, I'll stoutly set it again.

Bring me an old woman of fourscore years and ten,

Without a tooth in her head, I'll bring her young again.

The king observes:

"Thou be'st a noble doctor if that's all true thou be'st talking about."

And the doctor, taking to prose, replies:

"I'm not like those little mountebank doctors that go about the streets, and say this, that, and the other, and tell you as many lies in one half-hour as you would find in seven years; but what I does, I does clean before your eyes, and ladies and gentlemen, if you won't believe your own eyes, 'tis a very hard case."

The king agreeing that it is, the doctor goes to the patient, saying:

"I have a little bottle that I call golden foster drops. One drop on the root of this man's tongue and another on his crown, will strike the heat through his body, and raise him off the ground."

Accordingly the Turkish knight slowly rises and decamps, St. George exclaiming:

"Arise, arise, thou cowardly dog, and see how uprightly thou can'st stand. Go home into your own country and tell them what old England has done for you, and how they'll fight a thousand better men than you.

This last speech may have been added after the Crimean War, as the drama was copied out in 1857; but the staple of it was known long before, though with variations, in different villages, and it always concludes with little Johnny Jack, the smallest of the troup, with a bundle of dolls on his back, going round with a jingling money-box, saying:

Here comes I, little Johnny Jack,

Wife and family at my back,

My family's large though I am small,

And so a little helps us all.
Roast beef, plum pudding, strong beer and mince-pies,
Who loves that better than Father Christmas or I?
One mug of Christmas ale soon will make us merry and sing;
Some money in our pockets will be a very fine thing.
So, ladies and gentlemen, all at your ease,
Give the Christmas boys just what you please.

Before Christmas carols had to be reformed and regulated lest they should be a mere occasion of profanity and rudeness, that curious one of Dives and Lazarus was occasionally heard, of which two lines could never be forgotten -

He had no strength to drive them 'way,
And so they licked his sores.
And when Lazarus afterwards sees "Divers" "sitting on a serpent's knee."

May Day too survived in a feeble state, with the little voices singing:

April's gone! May's come!
Come and see our garland.

Mr. Keble improved the song into:

  April's gone, the king of showers,
  May is come, the queen of flowers,
  Give me something, gentles dear,
  For a blessing on the year.
  For my garland give, I pray,
  Words and smiles of cheerful May;
  Birds of spring, to you we come,
  Let us pick a little crumb.

In the dew of the morning we gathered our flowers
From the woodlands and meadows and garden bowers,
And now we have twisted our garland so gay,
We are come here to wish you a happy May Day.

We cannot but here add an outline of a village character from Old Times at Otterbourne:-

Mr. William Stainer was a baker. His bread was excellent, and he was also noted for what were called Otterbourne buns, the art of making which seems to have gone with him. They were small fair-complexioned buns, which stuck together in parties of three, and when soaked, expanded to twice or three times their former size. He used to send them once or twice a week to Winchester. But though baking was his profession, he did much besides. He was a real old-fashioned herbalist, and had a curious book on the virtues of plants, and he made decoctions of many kinds, which he administered to those in want of medicine. Before the Poor Law provided Union doctors, medical advice, except at the hospital, was almost out of reach of the poor. Mr. and Mrs. Yonge, like almost all other beneficent gentlefolks in villages, kept a medicine chest and book, and doctored such cases as they could venture on, and Mr. Stainer was in great favour as a practitioner, as many of our elder people can remember. He was exceedingly charitable and kind, and ready to give his help so far as he could. He was a great lover of flowers, and had contrived a sort of little greenhouse over the great oven at the back of his house, and there he used to bring up lovely geraniums and other flowers, which he sometimes sold. He was a deeply religious and devout man, and during an illness of the clerk took his place in Church, which was more important when there was no choir and the singers sat in the gallery. He was very happy in this office, moving about on felt shoes that he might make no noise, and most reverently keeping the Church clean, and watching over it in every way. He also continued in the post of schoolmaster, which at first he had only taken temporarily, and quaintly managing it. He was found setting as a copy "A blind man's wife needs no paint," which he defended as "Proverbs, sir, Proverbs." Giving up part of his business to his nephew, he still sat up at night baking, for the nephew, he said, was only in the A B C book of baking, and he also had other troubles: there was insanity in his family, and he was much harassed. His kindness and simplicity were sometimes abused. He never had the heart to refuse to lend money, or to deny bread on credit to hopeless debtors; and altogether debts, distress, baking, and watching his sisters all night, and school keeping all day, were too much for him. The first hint of an examination of his school completed the mischief and he died insane, drowning himself in the canal. It is a sad story, but many of us will remember with affectionate regard the good, kind, quaint, and most excellent little man.

A few lines, half parody, half original, may be added as picturing the old aspect of Otterbourne, about 1830:-

OLD REMEMBRANCES

I remember, I remember,
   Old times at Otterbourne,
Before the building of the Church,
   And when smock frocks were worn!

I remember, I remember,
   When railroads there were none,
When by stage coach at early dawn
   The journey was begun.
And through the turnpike roads till eve
   Trotted the horses four,
With inside passengers and out
   They carried near a score.
"Red Rover" and the "Telegraph,"
   We knew them all by name,
And Mason's and the Oxford coach,
   Full thirty of them came.
The coachman wore his many capes,
   The guard his bugle blew;
The horses were a gallant sight,
   Dashing upon our view.
I remember, I remember,
   The posting days of old;
The yellow chariot lined with blue
   And lace of colour gold.
The post-boys' jackets blue or buff,
   The inns upon the road;
The hills up which we used to walk
   To lighten thus the load.
The rattling up before the inn,
   The horses led away,
The post-boy as he touched his hat
   And came to ask his pay.
The perch aloft upon the box,
   Delightful for the view;
The turnpike gates whose keepers stood
   Demanding each his due.

I remember, I remember,
   When ships were beauteous things,
The floating castles of the deep
   Borne upon snow-white wings;
Ere iron-dads and turret ships,
   Ugly as evil dream,
Became the hideous progeny
   Of iron and of steam.
You crossed the Itchen ferry
   All in an open boat,
Now, on a panting hissing bridge
   You scarcely seem afloat.
Southampton docks were sheets of mud,
   Grim colliers at the quay.
No tramway, and no slender pier
   To stretch into the sea.
I remember, I remember,
   Long years ere Rowland Hill,
When letters covered quarto sheets
   Writ with a grey goose quill;
Both hard to fold and hard to read,
   Crossed to the scarlet seal;
Hardest of all to pay for, ere
   Their news they might reveal.
No stamp with royal head was there,
   But eightpence was the sum
For every letter, all alike,
   That did from London come!
I remember, I remember,
   The mowing of the hay;
Scythes sweeping through the heavy grass
   At breaking of the day.

The haymakers in merry ranks
   Tossing the swathes so sweet,
The haycocks tanning olive-brown
   In glowing summer heat.
The reapers 'mid the ruddy wheat,
   The thumping of the flail,
The winnowing within the barn
   By whirling round a sail.
Long ere the whirr, and buzz, and rush
   Became a harvest sound,
Or monsters trailed their tails of spikes,
   Or ploughed the fallow ground.
Our sparks flew from the flint and steel,
   No lucifers were known,
Snuffers with tallow candles came
   To prune the wick o'ergrown.
Hands did the work of engines then,
   But now some new machine
Must hatch the eggs, and sew the seams,
   And make the cakes, I ween.
I remember, I remember,
   The homely village school,
The dame with spelling book and rod,
   The sceptre of her rule.
A black silk bonnet on her head,
   Buff kerchief on her neck,
With spectacles upon her nose,
   And apron of blue check.
Ah, then were no inspection days,
   No standards then were known,
Children could freely make dirt pies,
   And learning let alone!

Those Sundays I remember too,
   When Service there was one;
For living in the parish then
   Of parsons there were none.
And oh, I can recall to mind,
   The Church and every pew;
William and Mary's royal arms
   Hung up in fullest view.
The lion smiling, with his tongue
   Like a pug dog's hung out;
The unicorn with twisted horn,
   Brooding upon his rout.
Exalted in the gallery high
   The tuneful village choir,
With flute, bassoon, and clarionet,
   Their notes rose high and higher.
They shewed the number of the Psalm
   In white upon a slate,
And many a time the last lines sung
   Of Brady and of Tate.
While far below upon the floor
   Along the narrow aisle,
The children on their benches sat
   Arranged in single file.
And there the clerk would stump along
   And strike with echoing blow
Each idle guilty little head
   That chattered loud or low.
Ah! I remember many things,
   Old, middle-aged, and new;
Is the new better than the old,
   More bright, more wise, more true?

The old must ever pass away,
   The new must still come in;
When these new things are old to you
   Be they unstained by sin.
So will their memory be sweet,
   A treasury of bliss
To be borne with us in the days
   When we their presence miss.
Trifles connected with the love
   Of many a vanished friend
Will thrill the heart and wake the sense,
   For memory has no end!

CHAPTER XVI - NATURAL HISTORY

Or animal life, though abundant, there is little or nothing special to record, besides the list of birds.

Polecats and martens only exist in the old rating book, but weasels and stoats remain, as well as a profusion of their prey - hares and rabbits. Squirrels haunt the trees, and otters are occasionally found in the river. Trout, grayling, now and then a pike, as well as the smaller fry of minnows and sticklebacks, are of course found in the streams. Eels used to be caught there on the moonlight nights by old labourers with a taste for sport, and the quaint little river crayfish may be picked out of the banks of the "water-carriages."

Toads and frogs are a matter of course. Sometimes a procession of tiny, but perfectly formed "Charley Frogs," as the village boys call them, just emerged from their tadpole state, may be seen making their way up from their native pools.

The pretty crested newt, dark brown and orange, with a gold crest along its back like an iguana, is found in shallow ponds, also the smooth newt. These efts, or evvets, as the people call them, are regarded with horror by the peasantry. The children speak of having seen one as if it were a crocodile; and an abscess in the arm has been ascribed to having picked up an "evvet in a bundle of grass."

The slow-worm, in silvery coat, is too often slaughtered as a snake. Vipers come to light in the woods, also the harmless brown snake. One of these has been seen swimming across a pond, his head just out of the water, another climbing an oak tree, and one, upon the lawn, was induced to disgorge a frog, which gathered up its legs and hopped away as if nothing had happened.

Of rats and mice and such small deer there are only too many, though it is worth while to watch rats at play round a hay-rick on Sunday evenings, when they know they will not be persecuted, and sit up like little kangaroos. The vole, which is not a rat, is a goodly sight, and the smooth round dormouse (or sleep-mouse, as the children call it) is a favourite gift imprisoned in an old tea-pot.

The beautiful nest of a field-mouse has been found in a cypress's thick foliage, and dead shrews bestrew the paths; though the magic effects of having a "sherry mouse" die in one's hand, and thus being enabled to stroke cattle and cure them, have never been experienced.

The anodon or fresh water mussel used to be found in Fisher's Pond on Colden Common, bordering on Otterbourne, and the green banks were strewn with shells left by the herons, but the pond is fast drying up and the herons have been driven away by guns.

The delicate paludina, of brown, horn-coloured, gracefully-formed shell, creeps on the water weeds, and hosts of snails may be studied.

Of insects less can be said here, but it is worth noting that one live purple emperor has been captured in Ampfield wood, two dead dilapidated ones picked up at Otterbourne.

The forest fly, so called, does not often come here; but it is observable that while strange horses are maddened by it, the native ones do not seem disturbed, knowing that it only creeps and does not bite. It is small and brown, not so formidable looking as the large fly, popularly called a stout, as big as a hornet, which lays eggs under the skin of cows.

But with the blue, green, and orange dragonflies of summer, this list must conclude, and turn to the birds and botany of the place, mostly well known, and verified by Mr. Townsend's Flora of Hampshire.

BIRDS

THE KITE (Milvus ictinus). - Sometimes hovering over heathlands or farmyards, but not very common.

SPARROW-HAWK (Accipiter fringillarius). - Taken in a trap set for rats at Otterbourne House.

PEREGRINE FALCON (Falco peregrinus), Hursley, 1857. - As a pair for many years had a nest on Salisbury spire, this one may have flown thus far.

KESTREL (Falco tinnunculus) - Otterbourne, 1856.

SHORT-EARED OWL (Otus brachyotus). - Baddesley Common, 5th March 1861.

WHITE OWL (Strix flammea). - Nested in a barn, another year in a pigeon-loft, and again in an old tub at Otterbourne. To be seen skimming softly along on summer evenings.

BROWN OWL (Ulula stridula). - Glides over the fields like a huge moth, and on moonlight nights in August may be heard the curious hunting note. As the eggs are hatched, not all at once, but in succession, a family taken out of a loft and put into a sea-kale pot were of various ages, the eldest nearly fledged, standing up as if to guard the nest, the second hissing and snapping, as if a naughty boy, and two downy infants who died. One brown owl was kept tame, and lived 14 years. The village people call this bird Screech Owl, and after a sudden death always mention having heard it.

CHIMNEY SWALLOW (Hirundo rustica). - They chase the flies under the bridges on the Itchen, and display their red throats.

HOUSE-MARTIN (Hirundo urbica). - Twittering everywhere 'neath the straw-built shed.

SAND-MARTIN (Hirundo riparia). - Swarms sit in rows along the electric wires, and bore deeply into every sand-pit.

SWIFT (Cypselus murarius). - First to come and first to go. Their peculiar screech and floating flight are one of the charms of the summer evenings.

NIGHTJAR (Caprimulgus europæus). - All through the twilight of the long days his purr-purr comes down from the heathery summit of Otterbourne Hill, where he earns his other name of Fern Owl, and may be seen flitting on silent wing in search of moths.

KINGFISHER (Alcedo ispida). - This beautiful creature darts out of the reeds bordering the Itchen, and it used to be at Chandler's Ford before the place was so populated. It seems also to haunt ponds or marshy places in woods, for a young full-fledged one was brought into Otterbourne House by a cat, alive and apparently unhurt. Another took a fancy to the gold-fish in a stone basin at Cranbury, and was shot, as the poor fish could not escape.

SPOTTED FLYCATCHER (Muscicapa grisola). - Late in summer these dainty little birds come whisking about the garden, perching on a rail, darting off after a fly, returning to the same post, or else feeding their young in nests on the side of the house. A pair built in 1897 in a flower-pot close to the window of Otterbourne House.

BUTCHER-BIRD (Lanius collurio). - Said to have been seen at Otterbourne. A slug has been found impaled on a thorn, but whether this was the shrike's larder, or as a charm for removing warts, is uncertain.

MISSEL-THRUSH (Merula viscivora). - This handsome bird is frequent, and commonly called House Screech. A story told by Warden Barter may be worth preserving. A pair of Missel Thrush seeing a peacock too near their nest, charged full at him, and actually knocked him down.

SONG-THRUSH (Merula musica). - Happily everywhere warbling on warm days in autumn and winter with a sweet, powerful song, some notes more liquid than even the nightingale's. The shells of the snails he has devoured bestrew the garden-walks.

BLACKBIRD (Merula vulgaris). - Out, with angry scream and chatter at the approach of an enemy, darts the "ousel cock so black of hue, with orange-tawny bill." How dull a lawn would be without his pert movements when he comes down alternately with his russet wife. One blackbird with a broad white feather on each side of his tail haunted Elderfield for two years, but, alas! one spring day a spruce sable rival descended and captivated the faithless dame. They united, chased poor Mr. Whitetail over the high garden hedge, and he was seen no more.

REDWING (Merula iliaca). - Not common, but noted by J. B. Y.

RING-OUZEL (Merula torquata). - Rare, but observed by J. B. Yonge in Otterbourne Park, 14th September 1865, and it has been seen several times later.

FIELDFARE (Merula pilaris). - In flocks in winter.

WHEATEAR (Sylvia ænanthe). - Comes to the downs.

STONECHAT (Saxicola rubicola). - Hops about on stones.

WHINCHAT (Saxicola rubetra). - On furze bushes on Otterbourne Hill.

REDBREAST (Sylvia rubecula). - A whole brood, two old and four young, used to disport themselves on the quilt of an old bedridden woman on Otterbourne Hill. It is the popular belief that robins kill their fathers in October, and the widow of a woodman declared that her husband had seen deadly battles, also that he had seen a white robin, but she possibly romanced.

REDSTART (Phænicura ruticilla). - Sometimes seen, but not often.

GRASSHOPPER-WARBLER (Salicaria locustella). - Well named, for it chirps exactly like a grasshopper in the laurels all through a summer evening.

SEDGE-WARBLER (Salicaria fragilis). - Whoever has heard it scolding and chattering in a ridiculous rage at a strange footstep will not wonder at the Scotch name of Blethering Jock. A pair nested in Dell Copse for some years, and the curious nest has been found among the reeds on the banks of the Itchen.

NIGHTINGALE (Sylvia luscinia). - Every year about the 18th of April the notes may be heard by the gate of Cranbury, in a larch wood on Otterbourne Hill, in the copse wood of Otterbourne House, at Oakwood, and elsewhere. For about a week there is constant song, but after nesting begins, it is less frequent. One year there was a nest in the laurels at Otterbourne House (since taken away), and at eight in the morning and seven at night the nightingale came on the lawn to feed, and was every morning chased by a surly John Bull of a robin. When the young are coming out of the nest the parents chide them, or strangers, in a peculiarly harsh chirp.

BLACKCAP (Sylvia atricapilla). - Fair and sweet, but not very frequent; nested in Dell Copse.

WHITETHROAT (Sylvia cinerea). - Darts about gardens, and is locally called Nettle-creeper.

LESSER WHITETHROAT (S. curruca). - Eggs in Dell Copse.

WOOD-WARBLER (Sylvia sylvicola). - Eggs taken at Cranbury.

WILLOW-WARBLER (Sylvia trochilus). - Eggs taken at Baddesley.

CHIEFCHAFF (Sylvia hippolaïs). - Common in spring.

GOLDEN-CRESTED WREN (Sylvia auricapilla). - A happy little inhabitant of the fir-trees, where it nests, and it is often to be seen darting in and out of a quickset hedge.

SKYLARK (Alauda arvensis). - The joy of eyes and ears in every open field. True to the kindred points of heaven and home.

WOODLARK (Alauda arborea). - Otterbourne Park and Cranbury.

YELLOW-BUNTING or YELLOW-HAMMER (Emberiza citrinella). - A great ornament, especially in autumn, when it sits on rails, crying, "A little bit of bread and no che-e-ese!"

BLACKHEADED or REED BUNTING (Emberiza schænidus). - Brambridge, April 1896.

SPARROW (Passer domesticus). - One curious fact about this despised animal is that the retired farmer, after whom Elderfield is named, made it his business to exterminate the village sparrows. He often brought them down to one, but always by the next morning that sparrow had provided himself with a mate to share his Castle Dangerous. Sparrows' (or sprows') heads make a figure in many church ratebooks.

CHAFFINCH (Fringilla cælebs). - Chink is the Hampshire name. The hens do not here migrate in winter, but a whole flight of them has been seen in the autumn on the Winchester road, evidently on their way; and once, after an early severe frost, about a hundred were found dead in a haystack near Basingstoke. Thomas Chamberlayne, Esq., who had a singular attraction for birds, used to have them coming to eat grain from his pocket. It has the perfection of a nest.

GOLDFINCH (Carduelis elegans). - This exquisite little bird is frequent on the borders of the chalk hills, where there is plenty of thistledown.

HAWFINCH (Coccothraustes vulgaris). - Sometimes seen, but not common.

LINNET (Linota cannabina). - Fairly frequent.

GREEN LINNET (Coccothraustes chloris). - Greenfinch, or Beanbird as they call it in Devonshire, is a pleasant visitor, though it has a great turn for pease.

WREN (Sylvia troglodytes). - This brisk little being Kitty Wren is to be seen everywhere. Whether Kingsley's theory is right that the little birds roll themselves into a ball in a hole in the winter, I know not. Single ones are certainly to be seen on a bank on a frosty, sunshiny day. Have they come out to view the world and report on it? Those very odd, unused nests are often to be found hanging from the thatch within outhouses. May it be recorded here that a wren once came to peck the sprigs on Miss Keble's gown?

GREAT TITMOUSE (Parus major) - or Ox-eye, as he is here called, bold and bright, crying "Peter" in early spring, and beautiful with his white cheek, and the black bar down his yellow waistcoat.

BLUE TIT (Parus cæruleus). - Bolder and prettier is the little blue-cap, a true sprite and acrobat as Wordsworth calls him.

MARSH-TIT (Parus palustris). - Known by less bright colouring and white breast.

COLE-TIT (Parus ater). - More grey, and very graceful. All these four will gladly come to a window in winter for a little fat hung to a string, and will put themselves into wonderful inverse positions.

LONG-TAILED TIT (Parus caudatus). - Long-tailed Caper, as is his local name, is more shy, and will not come to be fed; but the antics of a family after they have left their domed nest are delightful to watch, as they play in the boughs of a fir-tree.

HEDGE-SPARROW (Accentur modularis). - Quiet, mottled bird, to be seen everywhere.

PIED WAGTAIL (Motacilla lutor). - Most of these stay with us all winter, but one March evening at least forty-three descended on the lawn at Elderfield, doubtless halting in their flight from southern lands. Most winning birds they are, with their lively hop and jerking tails. Dish-washer is their Hampshire name.

GREY WAGTAIL (Motacilla boarula). - This pretty bird is really partly yellow. It is not very frequent here, but is sometimes found on the Itchen bank;

likewise the nest in a reedy meadow.

RAY'S WAGTAIL (Motacilla Rayi). - Ray's Wagtail was catching flies on a window at Otterbourne House in 1890.

TREE PITT (Anthus arboreus), MEADOW PIPIT (Anthus pratensis). - Small brown birds, not easy to distinguish; but the eggs differ, and both have been found.

BULLFINCH (Pyrrhula vulgaris). - It is charming to greet the black head and red waistcoat in the tops of the laurels or apple-trees, and surely this destroyer of insect devourers does more good than harm, if he does pick the buds to pieces in the search. He is a delightful pet, of exclusive and jealous attachments, hating every one except his own peculiar favourite; and his sober-coloured lady has quite as much character as he. One which was devoted to her own mistress would assail another of the family with such spite as sometimes to drive her out of the room.

STARLING (Sturnus vulgaris). - Green bedropped with gold when seen closely, but at a distance looking more like a rusty blackbird, though its gait on the lawn always distinguishes it, being a walk instead of a hop. Though not tuneful, no bird has such a variety of notes, and the clatter on the roof the call-note, the impatient summons of the brood about to be fed, make it a most amusing neighbour, when it returns to the same tree year after year.

RAVEN (Corvus corax). - He has flown over the village several times. One lived for many years in the yard of the George Inn at Winchester.

CROW (Corvus coronæ). - Game-preserving has nearly put an end to him, but he is seen round the folds on the downs in lambing time.

ROOK (Corvus frugilegus). - Shining and black the great birds come down on the fields. There is a rookery at Cranbury, another at Hams Farm at Allbrook, and a considerable one in the beeches near Merdon, for which the rooks deserted some oak-trees nearer the House. While these trees were still inhabited, Mr. G. W. Heathcote observed a number of walnuts under them, and found that the rooks brought them from the walnut avenues. A parliament of these wise birds is sometimes held on the downs, and there are woods where they assemble in great numbers in the autumn, contingents from all lesser rookeries pouring in to spend the winter, and whirling round and round in clouds before roosting.

JACKDAW (Corvus monedula). - A very amusing, though very wicked pet. There used to be throngs of them in the tower of the old church at Hursley, and their droll voices might be heard conversing in the evening. Mr. Chamberlayne had one which, after being freed, always came down to greet him when he walked in the garden.

MAGPIE (Corvus pica). - Pages might be filled with the merry mischief of this handsome creature. Perhaps the most observable characteristic of the three tame ones closely observed was their exclusive and devoted attachment to one person, whom they singled out for no cause that could be known, and followed about from place to place.

JAY (Garrulus glandarius). - May be heard calling in the pine plantations on Hursley Common. It would be as amusing as the magpie if tamed.

GREEN WOODPECKER (Picus viridis). - The laugh and the tap may be heard all through the Spring days. In 1890 Picus major, a small, black, and spotted French Magpie, as Devonians call it, was found, but we have no other right to claim it.

WRYNECK (Yunx torquilla), or Cuckoo's mate, squeaks all round the woods with his head on one side just as the cuckoo comes.

NUTHATCH (Sitta europæa). - This pretty creature will come and be fed on nuts at windows in the winter. These nuts he thrusts into crevices of bark to hold them fast while he hammers the shell. The remains may often be found. For many years a pair built in a hole half-way down an old apple-tree covered with ivy at Otterbourne House, and the exertions of the magpie with clipped wing to swing himself on a trail of ivy into the hole were comical, as well as his wrath when he fell off, as he uniformly did.

TREE-CREEPER (Certhia familiaris), winds round and round the trees like a little mouse.

HOOPOE (Upupa vulgaris). - Once in a frost caught alive by a shepherd on the downs, but it soon died.

CUCKOO (Cuculus canorus). - They cuckoo till "in June he altereth his tune." Probably the stammer is the effort of the young ones to sing. One grew up in a wagtail's nest in the flints that were built into the wall of Otterbourne Churchyard. Another, carried to the other side of the road and caged, was still fed by its foster-parents till it was ready to fly.

WOOD-PIGEON (Columba palumbus) -

Take two cows, Taffy,

Taffy, take two-o-o.

Plenty of this immoral exhortation may be heard in the trees. One young pigeon taken from the nest proved incorrigibly wild and ready to flutter to death whenever any one came near it.

TURTLE-DOVE (Columba turtur). - This pretty delicate creature with speckled neck builds in bushes lower than the wood-pigeon, and the mournful note resounds in the trees.

PHEASANT (Phasianus colchicus). - Not a real native, but cultivated to any extent. A cock pheasant with the evening sun gilding his back is a rare picture of beauty.

PARTRIDGE (Tetrao perdix). - Numerous.

HERON (Ardea cinerea). - Sometimes flies far overhead, the long legs projecting behind.

SANDPIPER (Totanus hypoleucus). - Seen walking over a mass of weeds in the Itchen canal.

SNIPE (Scolopax gallinago). - Brought in by sportsmen from the water meadows.

WOODCOCK (Scolopax rusticola). - Not common, but sometimes shot.

JACK-SNIPE (Scolopax gallinula). - Not common, but sometimes shot.

LAND-RAIL (Crex pratensis). - Corn-Crake. May be heard "craking" in the long grass in early morning before the hay is cut.

WATER-RAIL (Rallus aquaticus). - In a meadow at Otterbourne, 22nd January 1855.

LITTLE GREBE (Podiceps minor). - Dabchick, as it is commonly called, swims in the Itchen and in Fisher's Pond (on Colden Common), dipping down suddenly without a trace of the least alarm.

MOOR-HEN (Gallinula chloropus). - Very similar are the ways of the moor-hen, with its brilliant beak. But once, by some extraordinary chance, a moor-hen fell down a cottage chimney, and was brought alive for inspection by a boy, who, ignorant of natural objects, as was always the case in villages forty years ago, thought it a rare foreign specimen. It was a thatched cottage, but if it had been slated the moor-hen might have taken the roof for a sheet of water by moonlight, as the Great Water-Beetle has been known to do, and come down the chimney in like manner. A brood comes constantly to be fed on a lawn at Bishopstoke.

PEEWIT (Vanellus cristatus). - Otherwise the Crested Lapwing. It floats along in numbers when migrating, the whole flock turning at the same time and displaying either the dark or the white side of their wings with a startling effect. They seem effaced for a moment, the next the white sails are shown, then gone again. When paired, and nesting in the meadows, their cry causes their local name, as their other English title is derived from their characteristic manœuvres to lead the enemy from their young. Did they learn the habit when their so-called plovers' eggs became a dainty?

GOLDEN PLOVER (Charadrius pluvialis). - Noted at Otterbourne meadows by J. B. Yonge.

WILD DUCK (Anas boschas). - The mallard is splendid in plumage, and in shape is far more graceful than his domesticated brother. In early winter the wild ducks fly overhead in a wedge-shaped phalanx, and by and by they pair, and if disturbed start up with a sudden quack, quack from the copse-wood pond. Broods of downy wild ducks have been brought in by boys, but it has almost always proved impossible to rear them.

TEAL (Querquedula anas). - This very pretty little duck used to build on Cranbury Common, but may have been frightened away by increasing population.

GULL (Larus canus). - Flocks of those white-breasted birds sometimes alight on ploughed fields round Otterbourne, and even some miles farther from the sea. They are sometimes kept in gardens to destroy the slugs.

These birds have all been actually seen and noted down by members of the Yonge family.

FLOWERS

TRAVELLER'S JOY (Clematis Vitalba). - Locally called Old Man's Beard, most appropriately, as its curling, silvery masses of seeds hang in wreaths over the hedges. There is a giant trunk growing up from the moat of Merdon Castle.

MEADOW RUE (Thalictrum flavum). - Handsome foliage and blossoms, showing much of anthers, growing on the banks of the Itchen canal.

WINDFLOWER (Anemone nemorosa). - Smellfoxes, as the villagers' children inelegantly term this elegant flower, spreading its pearl-white blossom, by means of its creeping root, all over the copses, and blushing purple as the season advances.

WATER CROWFOOT (Ranunculus aquatilis). - The white flowers, with yellow eyes, make quite a sheet over the ponds of Cranbury Common, etc. Ivy-leaved (R. hederaceus). - Not so frequent. The ivy-shaped leaves float above, the long fibrous ones go below. When there is lack of moisture, leaves and flower are sometimes so small that it has been supposed to be a different species. It was once in a stagnant pond in Boyatt Lane, but is extinct again.

BUTTERCUP or CROWFOOT -

(R. sceleratus) Highly-polished petals, which spangle

(R. acris) the fields and hedges with gold.

(R. repens) All much alike; all haunting

(R. bulbosus) kitchen-gardens and pastures, where the cattle, disliking their taste, leave the stems standing up alone.

SPEARWORT (R. flammula). - Flower like the others, but with narrow leaves.

GOLDILOCKS (R. auricomus). - More delicate, upper leaves spear-shaped, lower pinnate. In the borders of the copse wood of Otterbourne House.

CORN CROWFOOT (R. Ficaria). - Small, growing between the corn with hooked capsules.

SMALL CELANDINE (R. Bcaria). - The real buttercup of childhood, with its crown of numerous shining petals, making stars along the banks at the first breath of spring. One of the most welcome of flowers.

KING CUPS (Caltha palustris). - Large, gorgeous flowers, in every wet place, making a golden river in a dell at Cranbury.

GREEN HELLEBORE (Helleborus viridis). - Under an oak-tree, in a hedgerow leading from King's Lane, Standon, and in Hursley.

FUMITORY (Fumaria officinalis). - The pretty purple blossoms and graceful bluish foliage often spring up in gardens where they are treated as weeds.

YELLOW F. (F. lutea). - An old wall at Hursley.

CLIMBING F. (Corydalis claviculata). - Cuckoo bushes. Standon, and in Hursley.

COLUMBINE (Aquilegia vulgaris). - This group of purple doves, or of Turkish slippers, does not here merit the term vulgaris, though, wherever it occurs, it is too far from a garden to be a stray. Ampfield Wood, Lincoln's Copse, King's Lane, and Crabwood have each furnished a specimen.

BARBERRY (Berberis vulgaris). - This handsome shrub of yellow wood, delicate clusters of yellow flowers, and crimson fruit in long oval bunches has been sedulously banished from an idea that it poisons grass in its vicinity. There used to be a bush in Otterbourne House grounds, but it has disappeared, and only one now remains in the hedge of Pitt Downs.

POPPY (Papaver Rhæas). - Making neglected fields glorious with a crimson mantle, visible for miles in the sun.

GREATER CELANDINE (Chelidonium majus). - Yellow flowers, very frail, handsome pinnate leaf - lane at Brambridge, Standon, and in Hursley.

CRUCIFERA

ROCKET (Diplotaxis tenuifolia). - Seen at Brambridge.

CHARLOCK (Sinapis arvensis). - Making fields golden.

WHITE C. (S. alba). - Standon, Hursley.

JACK-BY-THE-HEDGE (Sisymbrium alliaria). - Seen at Brambridge.

LADY'S SMOCK (Cardamine pratensis). - No doubt named because the pearly flowers look on a moist meadow like linen bleaching. Sometimes double in rich ground.

HAIRY CARDAMINE (C. hirsuta). - Hursley.

YELLOW ROCKET (Barbarea vulgaris). - Road near Chandler's Ford. Near bridge over Itchen.

WATERCRESS (Nasturtium officinale). - Everywhere in running water, and now Poolhole is made into a nursery for it.

SHEPHERD'S PURSE (Thlaspi Bursa-pastoris). - Even the purses are to be seen before we well know the tiny white flowers to be in blossom.

PENNYCRESS (T. arvense). - Larger, and uplifting a spike of rounded, fan-shaped capsules.

WILD MIGNONETTE (Reseda lutea). - Mignonette all but the perfume - chalk-pits.

DYER'S ROCKET (R. luteola). - Slenderer and more spiked; more common.

ROCK ROSE (Helianthemum vulgare). - There is an elegance and delicacy of colour about this little cistus which renders it one of the most charming of the many stars of the wayside, as it grows on Compton Hill.

SWEET VIOLET (Viola odorata). - The colour, purple or white or pink, seems to depend on the soil. White are the most common on the chalky side, blue on the gravel.

MARSH V. (V. palustris). - Small and pale, with round leaves. Seen at a spring in Otterbourne Park. (V. permixta). - Pinky - Kiln-yard, Otterbourne.

DOG V. (V. canina). - In every wood, rich and handsome.

SNAKE V. (V. hirta). - More delicate and small, growing in turf - Pleasure Grounds, Cranbury.

(V. Riviniana). - Hursley Park.

(V. Reichenbachiana). - Dane Lane. The three last are very probably only sports of canina.

CREAM-COLOURED V. (V. lactea). - More skim-milk coloured, but known by lanceolate leaves - cuckoo bushes.

PANSY (V. tricolor). - Everywhere in fallow fields. In rich soil the upper petals become purple.

SUNDEW -

(Drosera rotundifolia) The curious, hairy, dewy leaves

(D. intermedia) and flowers that never open in full day are to be found in the marshes near Hiltingbury.

MILKWORT (Polygala vulgaris). - Small and blue on Otterbourne Hill, as a stitch in the embroidery of the turf; but larger, blue, pink, or white in the water-meadows beside the Itchen, deserving the American name of May-wings.

CARYOPHYLLEÆ

DEPTFORD PINK (Dianthus Armeria). - This used to grow in a field near Highbridge, but has been destroyed, either purposely or by fencing.

BLADDER CAMPION (Silene inflata). - Showing its white flowers and swelling calyxes everywhere.

COMMON CATCHFLY (S. anglica). - Small and insignificant among corn.

RED CAMPION (Lychnis diurna). - Robins, as children call it, with the bright pink in every hedge and the undergrowth in every copse.

WHITE C. (L. vespertina). - The white flowers make a feature in fallow fields.

RAGGED ROBIN (L. Flos-cuculi). - The curiously slashed and divided pink flowers flourish in the water-meadows by the Itchen.

CORN COCKLE (Agrostemma githago). - The beautiful purple blossoms, set in long graceful calyxes, adorn the paths through wheat and barley fields everywhere.

LESSER STITCHWORT (Mænchia erecta). -

CHICKWEED -

(Cerastiurn vulgatum) Early plant. Uninteresting

(C. arvense) tiny white flowers.

STARWORT (Stellaria Holostea). - The bright stitches of white embroidery on our banks.

CHICKWEED (S. media.) - The chickweed dear to bird-keepers.

(S graminea). - Cobweb-like, almost invisible stems, and blossom with a fairy brightness over the heaths.

(S. uliginosa). - The same adapted to marshes - Cuckoo Bushes, Helmsley.

SANDWORT (Arenaria Rubra). - The little pink flowers crop up through the gravel paths.

CORN SPURREY (Spergula arvensis). - Very long-spurred, with white small blossoms.

(Alsine tenuifolia). - Roman road between Hursley and Sparsholt.

KNAWEL (Scleranthus annuus). - Hursley.

ST. JONN'S-WORT TRIBE

TUTSAN (Hypericum Androsæmum). - Handsome flower, and seeds - Cranbury and Allbrook.

ST. JOHN'S-WORT (H. perforatum).

(H. dubium).

(H. hirsutum). - All frequent in the hedges.

(H. humifusum).

(H. pulchrum).

(H. Elodes). - Bogs near Cuckoo Bushes.

(H. quadrangulum).

MALLOW (Malva sylvestris). - Everywhere by roadsides, used to be esteemed by old women as a healing "yarb."

MUSK M. (M. moschata). - A beautiful pink or white flower, grows all over the park at Cranbury.

DWARF M. (M. rotundifolia). - Flower white, with purple streaks, almost stemless, grows under a wall in Otterbourne Street.

SMALL-LEAVED LIME (Tilia parvifolia). - Hursley Park; avenue at Brambridge, where four rows form three magnificent aisles.

CRANESBILL TRIBE

DOVE'S-FOOT CRANE'S-BILL (Geranium Columbinum). - Roadsides.

SHINING C. (G. lucidum). - Heap of stones, Hursley.

(G. dissectum). - Everywhere.

(G. Molle). - Otterbourne

HERB ROBERT C. (G. Robertianum). - Very common, and the crimson leaves a great winter ornament.

BLOODY C. (G. phæum). - Ladwell Hill, where it may be a remnant of a cottage garden.

STORK'S-BILL (Erodium moschatum). - Otterbourne Hill.

(E. cicutarium). - Farley Mount.

WOOD-SORREL (Oxalis Acetosella). - This exquisite plant with delicate flower and trefoil leaves grows on many mossy banks, especially on one on the Ampfield Road.

HOLLY (Ilex Aquifolium). - The glory of the peaty woods. The people distinguish the berried shrubs as holly, i.e. holy, those without berries being holm.

SPINDLE-TREE (Euonymus europæus). - Also called skewer wood. "A tree that grows on purpose," as an old woman said of the material of her pegs. The charming berries with their crimson hearts are plentiful in King's Lane.

BUCKTHORN (Rhamnus Frangula). - Otterbourne Hill.

(R. catharticus) . - Hursley.

SYCAMORE (Acer Pseudo-platanus). - Road by Oakwood.

MAPLE (A. campestre). - Painting the hedges in autumn with its yellow leaves.

LEGUMINOSE

FURZE (Ulex europæus). - Brilliant on all the commons on gravel or peat.

DWARF FURZE (U. nanus) - Rather less frequent.

BROOM (Genista scoparia). - Exquisite golden spires on the peat.

NEEDLE BROOM (G. anglica). - Cuckoo Bushes.

DYER'S GREENWEED (G. tinctoria). - In a ditch in a meadow on the Ampfield Road.

REST HARROW (Ononis arvensis). - Pretty pink and white blossoms like miniature lady-peas on a troublesome weed.

KIDNEY VETCH (Anthyllis Vulneraria) . - Borders of down.

BLACK MEDICK (Medicago lupulina). - Chalk-pit.

(M. denticulata) . - Ampfield.

MELILOT (Melilotus officinalis). - Kiln Lane, Otterbourne.

BIRDSFOOT (Ornithopus perpusillus). - Otterbourne Hill.

(Trigonella ornithopodioides). - Otterbourne.

TREFOIL (Trifulium subterraneum).

(T. pratense).

DUTCH CLOVER (T. repens).

HOPDOWN (T. procumbens).

(T. minus).

(T. hybridum).

STRAWBERRY TREFOIL (T. fragiferum). - Once on canal bank.

MILK VETCH (Hippocrepis comosa). - Hursley.

BIRD'S-FOOT TREFOIL (Lotus corniculatus). - This golden or ruddy part of the embroidery of the down is known to children as Ladies' Slippers or Ladies' Fingers.

(L. major). - A taller variety.

TARE (Ervum hirsutum). - Tiny grey flowers.

(E. tetraspermum).

PURPLE VETCH (Vicia Cracca). - Throwing royal purple garlands over every hedge in the lanes.

COMMON V. (V. sativa). - Very common, varying from crimson to dark red.

WOOD V. (V. sepium). - A brilliant little red flower.

GRASS VETCHLING (Lathyrus Nissolia). - Found once in a bank near Chandler's Ford; once at Silkstede.

WOOD V. (L. sylvestris). - Doubtful, but something like it grows in Sparrow Grove near the waterworks.

YELLOW V. (L. pratensis). - Common, mixed with grass.

HEATH PEA (Orobus tuberosus). - On the peat soil.

ROSE TRIBE

BLACKTHORN (Prunus spinosa). - It is believed that no hurt is so hard of healing as from a blackthorn. Also blackthorn winter is supposed to bring fresh cold in spring, when the bushes almost look as if clothed by hoar-frost.

WILD CHERRY (P. Avium). - The fine, tall, shapely trees put on their bridal show in the woods of Cranbury and Ampfield.

BIRD-CHERRY (P. Padus). - Not very common. There is one in the grounds at Otterbourne House, but it is not certainly wild.

MEADOW-SWEET (Spiræa Ulmaria). - Raising its creamy cymes of blossoms in every ditch where there is a little moisture.

DROPWORT (S. Filipendula). - On the borders of Pitt Down and Crab Wood.

AGRIMONY (Agrimonia Eupatoria). - Long yellow spikes in all dry hedges.

BURNET (Sanguisorba officinalis). - Chalk-pit by Sparrow Grove, also Dane Lane, where the green balls with tiny red blossoms may be found, and sometimes the green and crimson burnet moth.

BARREN STRAWBERRY (Potentilla Fragariastrum). - How often has "mustn't pick the strawberry blossom" been quoted to this delusive little white cinquefoil in early spring, when it peeps out among leaves very like strawberry-leaves in the hedge.

TORMENTIL (P. Tormentilla). - This is now ranged among the cinquefoils, though it has only four petals, owing perhaps to the very dry barren heathy soil it brightens with its stars.

CINQUEFOIL (P. repens). - A smiling pentagon star by the wayside.

SILVER-WEED or GOOSE-GRASS (P. anserina). - Why dedicated to geese, even in Latin, it is hard to say. Silver-weed is more appropriate to the silver-grey leaves that border road-sides, sometimes with golden flowers.

MARSH CINQUEFOIL (Comarum palustre). - A prize in Baddesley bog, unless drains have banished its pure flower.

WOOD STRAWBERRY (Fragaria vesca). - Profuse in Cranbury and on banks of railway at Sparrow Grove.

WILD RASPBERRY (Rubus Idæus). - Cranbury, near the road.

WILD BLACKBERRY (R. fruticosus). - Brambles, of course, everywhere, but it is impossible to pass them without a tribute to their beauty, in flower, in fruit, and, above all, in autumn foliage.

DEWBERRY (R. cæsius). - What is probably dewberry grows by the roadway through Mallibar Copse.

(R. leucostratus). - Roman Road and Cranbury Common.

HERB BENNET (Geum urbanum). - Insignificant yellow flower.

WATER AVENS (G. rivale). - Quaint little ruddy half-expanded blossoms, called by the villagers Granny's Night-caps.

(G. intermedium). - Really intermediate - probably hybrid. Found once in a copse between Boyatt Lane and the Southampton Road.

LADY'S MANTLE (Alchemilla arvensis). - Crabwood.

SWEET-BRIAR (Rosa rubiginosa). - Copse by pond, Cranbury.

DOG-ROSE (R. canina). - With handsomer hips.

WHITE DOG-ROSE (R. arvensis).

HAWTHORN (Cratægus monogyna). - Who does not love when the blossoms cover them like snow-drift? Well are they called May.

MOUNTAIN ASH (Pyrus Aucuparia). - This rowan-tree of Scotland has no weird horrors here, but it is the ornament of the woods, with white cymes, red berries, and feathery leaves.

CRAB-TREE (P. Malus). - Romsey Road, where the pinky blossoms show opposite Cranbury Gate.

WHITEBEAM (P. Aria). - Grey or white leaves shine out in Ampfield Wood.

PURPLE LOOSESTRIFE (Lythrum salicaria). - Ophelia's long purples adorn the water-courses in the Itchen mead.

WILLOW-HERB TRIBE

ROSEBAY WILLOW-HERB (Epilobium angustifolium). - This splendid flower, rose-coloured, white-pistilled and red-leaved, spreads in sheets in Cranbury Copse and on railway cuttings, at Cuckoo Bushes, and in Ampfield Wood.

CODLINS-AND-CREAM (E. hirsutum). - Adorning wet places.

SMALL WILLOW-HERB -

(E. parvaeorurn) Troublesome though pretty weeds in the garden.

(E. tetragonum)

(E. roseum)

(E. montanum). - Found at Ampfield.

ENCHANTER'S NIGHTSHADE (Circæa lutetiana). - A graceful, delicate-looking plant of universal occurrence.

WATER STARWORT (Callitriche verna). - Ponds.

MARESTAIL (Hippuris vulgaris). - Waves with the current of the stream in the Itchen.

WHITE BRYONY (Bryonia dioica). - Vine-like leaves wreathe round in the hedges, and the pale, whitish flowers give place to graceful clusters of red berries.

GOOSEBERRY (Ribes Grossularia). - Lane towards Brambridge.

SAXIFRAGEA

ORPINE (Sedum Telephium). - Also called Midsummer May; grows in Otterbourne Park, and a large bunch on the Romsey Road. An old woman described having tried the augury, having laid the plants in pairs on Midsummer Eve, naming them after pairs of sweethearts. Those that twisted away from each other showed inconstancy!

STONECROP (S. anglicum). - Otterbourne Hill.

(S. acre). - Hursley.

HOUSELEEK (Sempervivum tectorum). - Also called Sin-green, or some word so sounding. It is not permitted to blow upon the roof on which it grows, for fear of ill-luck, which is strange, as it has been Jupiter's beard, Thor's beard, and St. George's beard, and in Germany is thought to preserve from thunder.

SAXIFRAGE (Saxifraga tridactylites). - Hursley.

GOLDEN S. (Chrysosplenium oppositifolium). - Wet places in Lincoln's Copse.

MARSH PENNYWORT (Hydrocotyle vulgaris). - Bogs at Cuckoo Bushes.

WOOD SANICLE (Sanicula vulgaris). - In all the copses.

UMBELLIFERA

GOUTWEED (Ægopodium Podagra). - Handsome leaves, but a troublesome weed.

PIGNUT (Bunium flexuosum). - The delicate, lace-like, umbellate flowers in all the woods.

WATER DROPWORT (Œnanthe fistulosa). - Banks of Itchen.

WATER HEMLOCK (Œ. crocata). - Itchen banks.

WILD CARROT (Daucus Carota).

BURNET SAXIFRAGE (Pimpinella Sax Jraga). - Hursley.

COW PARSLEY (Chærophyllum sylvestre). - Boys may be seen bearing home bundles for their rabbits.

SHEPHERD'S NEEDLE (Scandix Pecten Veneis). - In cornfields.

HEDGE PARSLEY (Torilis infesta). - Hursley.

HEMLOCK (Conium maculatum).

IVY (Hedera Helix). - Everywhere.

DOGWOOD (Cornus sanguinea). - The red and purple of the fading leaves mixed with the yellow of the maples make every hedge a study.

MISTLETOE (Viscum album). - Grows on hawthorns in Hursley Park, and on apple-trees at Otterbourne.

MOSCATEL (Adoxa Moschatellina). - This dainty little green-headed plant is one of the harbingers of spring.

ELDER (Sambucus nigra). - In most hedges, though its honours are gone as the staple of elder-wine, and still better of elder-flower water, which village sages used to brew, and which was really an excellent remedy for weak eyes.

GUELDER-ROSE (Viburnum Opulus). - Equally handsome whether white-garlanded cymes of blossoms or scarlet berries, waxen when partly ripe.

WAYFARING-TREE (V. Lantana). - Not quite so common, but handsome, with white flowers and woolly leaves.

HONEYSUCKLE (Lonicera Periclymenum). - To be seen in full glory waving on the top of a holly-tree, and when the stem has become amalgamated with a bough, circling it like the staff of Esculapius, it is precious to boys.

(L. Caprifolium). - Noted as once found, but not lately.

MADDER TRIBE

MADDER (Rubia peregrina). - Tiny flowers - Otterbourne Hill.

CROSSWORT or MUGWORT (Galium Cruciatum). - Roadside, Allbrook.

YELLOW LADY'S BEDSTRAW (G. verum). - Everywhere.

MARSH B. (G. palustre). - Cuckoo Bushes.

(G. uliginosum). - Gravel-pit, Otterbourne.

WHITE BEDSTRAW (G. erectum). - Winchester Road.

CLEAVERS or CLIDERS (G. Aparine). - Everywhere.

ROUGH (G. Mollugo). - Cornfields.

WOODRUFF (Asperula odorata). - Sparrow Grove.

(A. cynanchica). - Chalk downs.

FIELD MADDER (Sherardia arvensis). - Otterbourne Hill.

VALERIAN (Valeriana dioica). - Itchen meadows.

LESSER V. (V. officinalis). - Itchen meadows.

LAMB'S LETTUCE (Valerianella olitorium). - Downs and stubble-fields.

TEASEL (Dipsacus sylvestris). - Grand ornament to the hedges. On a fallow field it came up in quantities, as if sown.

DEVIL'S-BIT SCABIOUS (Scabiosa succisa). - Makes grey clouds all over Cranbury Park.

COMMON S. (S. arvensis). - Everywhere.

LESSER S. (S. Columbaria). - Malabar wayside.

HARE BELL (Campanula rotundifolia). - Otterbourne Hill.

NETTLE-LEAVED BELLFLOWER (C. Trachelium). - Road-sides.

CLUSTERED B. (C. glomerata). - Pitt Down.

COMPOSITÆ

THISTLES (Carduus nutans).

(C. tenuifolia).

MILK THISTLE (Silybum marianum). - Once in Boyatt Lane.

(S crispus).

(Cnicus lanceolatus).

(C. palustris).

(C. arvensis).

STEMLESS T. (C. acaulis). - Little purple stars on the downs.

CARLINE (Carlina vulgaris).

BURDOCK (Arctium Lappa). - Everywhere.

(A. tomentosa).

SAW-WORT (Serratula tinctoria). - Copses round King's Lane.

KNAPWEED (Centaurea nigra). - Everywhere.

(C. Cyanea). - In fields about Hursley occasionally.

(C. Scabiosa). - Hursley.

CORN MARIGOLD (Chrysanthemum segetum). - Sometimes plentiful, but dependent on crops.

OX-EYE DAISY (C. Leucanthemum). - Everywhere.

CAMOMILE (Pyrethrum inodorum). - Everywhere.

TANSY (Tanacetum vulgaris). - King's Lane.

COMMON CHAMOMILE (Anthemis nobilis).

(A. arvensis).

(A. Cotula).

YARROW (Achillea Millefolium).

SNEEZEWORT (A. Ptarmica). - Southampton Road sides.

WORMWOOD (Artemisia vulgaris). - Kiln Lane turns to Moat House.

CUDWEED (Gnaphalium minimum).

(G. germanium).

(G. sylvaticum).

GROUNDSEL (Senecio vulgaris).

(S. sylvaticus).

RAGWORT (S. Jacobæa). - Often covered with black and yellow caterpillars.

(S. viscosus). - Marked as found at Hursley.

(S. aquaticus).

FLEABANE (Inula Conyza). - Southampton Road.

(I. Pulicaria).

DAISY (Bellis perennis).

BLUE FLEABANE (Erigeron acris).

GOLDENROD (Solidago Virga-aurea). - Wood-paths and road-sides.

COLTSFOOT (Tussilago Farfara). - In all chalky fields.

BUTTERBUR (Petasites vulgaris). - Banks of Itchen.

BUR-MARIGOLD (Bidens cernua). - It used to be in a marsh on the Romsey Road, but has not been seen lately.

HEMP AGRIMONY (Eupatorium cannabinum). - In all hedges near moisture.

CHICORY (Cichorium Intybus). - Now and then showing its pretty blue flower on the roadside.

NIPPLEWORT (Lapsana communis). - Too frequent weed.

DANDELION (Leontodon Taraxacum). - How can its praise for glorious brilliant flowers and stems fit for chains be passed by, or for the "clocks" that furnish auguries!

(L. autumnalis). - Is this a separate species, or the dandelion blowing in autumn?

GO-TO-BED AT NOON (Tragopogon pratensis). - Beautiful when open early in the day, beautiful when the long calyx is closed, and most beautiful with its handsome winged pappus - King's Lane, Otterbourne Churchyard.

WILD LETTUCE (Lactuca muralis). - On heaps of flints.

MOUSEAR (Thrincia hirta). - Sulphur-coloured, small, and held to be an excellent remedy for whooping-cough.

OX-TONGUE (Helminthia echioides). - The rough leaf is well named.

HAWKBIT (Hieracium autumnale).

(Apargia hispida). - In cornfields.

SHEEP'S-BIT (Jasione montana). - Cranbury Common.

SOW THISTLE (Sonchus arvensis).

(S. palustris).

WHORTLEBERRY (Vaccinium Myrtillus). - Ampfield Wood.

CROSS-LEAVED HEATH (Erica Tetralix) Otterbourne Hill, the glory of early autumn.

BELL HEATHER (E. cinerea).

LING (Calluna vulgaris)

BIRD'S NEST (Monotropa Hypopitys). - South Lynch Wood.

ASH (Fraxinus excelsior).

PRIVET (Ligustrum vulgare). - Lane leading to the Itchen.

GENTIAN TRIBE

THE PERIWINKLE (Vinca minor). - Curiously irregular in blossoming. One spring the ground is covered with blue stars, another only with evergreen trails. Its only habitat here is Lincoln's Copse.

YELLOWWORT (Chlora perfoliata). - Ampfield Wood.

CENTAURY (Erythræa Centaurea). - Cranbury.

GENTIAN (Gentiana Pneunomanthe). - Baddesley bog, Cranbury.

(G. Amarella). - Pitt Down.

BOGBEAN (Menyanthes trifolium). - This lovely flower abides in the wet banks of the Itchen.

BINDWEED (Convolvulus sepium). - Pure and white.

(C. minor). - In shades of pink. Called lilies by the country-folk.

DODDER (Cuscuta Epithymum). - Red threads forming a beaded network over the furze.

(C. Trifolii). - Coarser fibres, smaller balls of blossom, in some years strangling the clover.

WOODY NIGHTSHADE (Solanum Dulcamara). - Purple flowers, red berries, beautiful everywhere.

(S. nigrum). - White-flowered, black-berried. At Cranbury, and occasionally elsewhere.

DEADLY NIGHTSHADE (Atropa belladonna). - Used to be near the front door at Hursley Park.

HENBANE (Hyoscyamus niger). - Formerly on the top of Compton Hill, and at the angle of the lane leading to Bunstead.

BORAGE TRIBE

MULLEIN (Verbascum nigrum). The handsome spikes

(V. Thapsus) everywhere.

(V. Blattaria). - Formerly in hedge of cottage at Silkstede.

GROMWELL (Lithospermum officinale). - Beside Winchester Road on way to Twyford.

FORGET-ME-NOT (Myosotis palustris). - Itchen meadows.

MOUSE-EAR, SCORPION GRASS (M. versicolor). - Stubblefields.

(M. sylvatica). - Ampfield.

(M. arvensis). - Everywhere.

COMFREY (Symphytum officinale). - Itchen banks.

HOUND'S TONGUE (Cynoglossum officinale). - Merdon Hill, but it has disappeared from Otterbourne.

PRIMROSE (Primula vulgaris). - Has any one observed the tiny blossoms of seedlings of the first year? Now and then there are stalked heads like oxlips, white or red varieties.

COWSLIP (P. veris). - Covering some few fields, and delightful for cowslip balls. Sweetest of scents.

YELLOW LOOSESTRIFE (Lysimachia vulgaris). - A beautiful shrub by the water-side.

MONEYWORT (L. Nummularia). - The Creeping-Jenny of rock-work, etc.

YELLOW PIMPERNEL (L. nemorum). - Covering the ground in woods with its delicate pentagon stars.

PIMPERNEL (Anagallis arvensis). - A beautiful blue variety once came up in the kitchen-garden at Otterbourne House, and prevailed for several years.

(A. tenella). - In the bogs towards Cuckoo Bushes.

LABIATÆ

WATER FIGWORT -

(Scrophularia Balbisii). Both common and not beautiful.

(S. nodosa)

FOXGLOVE (Digitalis purpurea). - All over the gravelly and peaty woods in splendid congregations of spires - called by the children poppies.

LESSER SNAPDRAGON (Antirrhinum Orontium). - Occasionally in gardens.

WILD SAGE (Salvia Verbenaca). - Ampfield.

SELF-HEAL (Prunella vulgaris). - Called Lady's Slipper.

SKULLCAP (Scutellaria galericulata). - Itchen bank.

(S. minor). - Cranbury hedge on Romsey Road.

BLACK HOREHOUND (Bellota fætida). - Hursley hedges.

BASTARD BALM (Melittis Melissophyllum). - Ampfield Wood.

BETONY (Stachys Betonica).

(S. palustris).

(S. sylvatica).

(S. arvensis).

RED ARCHANGEL (Galeopsis Tetrahit). - Near Chandler's Ford.

MOTHERWORT (Leonurus Cardiaca). - Alas, a dried specimen only remains of this handsome flower, which was sacrificed to a pig-stye on Otterbourne Hill.

WEASEL SNOUT or YELLOW NETTLE (Galeobdolon luteum).

WHITE ARCHANGEL, or BLIND NETTLE (Lamium album). - sometimes with a purple flower.

(L. purpureum). - Everywhere.

BUGLE (Ajuga reptans). - All over the woods.

GERMANDER, WOOD-SAGE (Teucrium Scorodonia). - Cranbury Wood.

BUGLOSS (Lycopsis arvensis). - Sand-pit, Boyatt Lane.

VIPER'S BUGLOSS (Echium vulgare). - Chalk-pits.

GREAT YELLOW TOADFLAX (Linaria vulgaris). - In most hedges.

IVY-LEAVED T. (L. Cymbalaria). - Old wall of Merdon Castle.

FLUELLEN (L. Elatine). - In stubble-fields.

(L. spuria). - In the same locality.

CREEPING T. (L. repens). - Chandler's Ford, and hedge of Romsey Road by Pot Kiln.

LESSER T. (L. minor). - Hursley.

SPEEDWELL (Veronica hederifolia). - Hursley, Ampfield.

(V. polita).

(V. Buxbaumii). - In fallow fields all the winter and spring.

(V. arvensis).

(V. officinalis). - Cranbury.

BIRD'S EYE (V. Chamvdrys). - Exquisite blue along the hedges on the chalk and clay.

(V. montana). - Ampfield.

(V. scutellata).

BROOKLIME (V. Beccabunga). - Esteemed a sovereign remedy for an old woman's bad leg.

(V. Anagallis). - Less common, but both frequent the river and the marshes.

EYEBRIGHT (Euphrasia officinalis). - Downs and heaths.

RED EYEBRIGHT (Bartsia Odontites). - woods.

RED RATTLE (Pedicularis palustris). - Itchen meadows.

(P. sylvatica). - Otterbourne Hill.

YELLOW RATTLE (Rhinanthus Crista-galli). - Itchen meadows.

YELLOW COW-WHEAT (Melampyrum pratense). - Otterbourne Park.

TOOTHWORT (Lathræa squamaria). - South Lynch Wood.

BROOMRAPE (Orobanche repens). - Mallibar roadway.

(O. elatior). - Sparrow Grove.

(O. minor). - Clover-fields, Otterbourne. Wonderful brown parasites, all three.

VERVEIN (Verbena officinalis). - Road-sides.

GIPSYWORT (Lycopus europærus). - Dell Copse and all bogs.

HORSE MINT (Mentha sylvestris).

(M. hirsuta).

(M. sativa).

(M. arvensis).

THYME (Thymus Serpyllum). - On many a bank does the wild thyme grow, with its perfume delicious.

MARJORAM (Origanum vulgare). - Banks of Winchester Road.

MONKEY FLOWER (Mimulus Luteus) - Bank of Itchen Canal, where it has spread considerably, though probably a stray.

BASIL THYME (Calamintha vulgaris). - Stubble-fields show this lovely little blue flower with a white crescent on the lip.

(C. menthifolia). - Merdon Castle.

BASIL (C. Clinopodium). - Itchen.

CAT MINT (Nepeta Cataria). - Hedge towards Stoneham.

GROUND IVY (N. Glechoma). - Everywhere in woods.

PLANTAIN TRIBE

KNOCKHEADS (Plantago major).

LESSER PLANTAIN (P. media).

(P. lanceolata).

STAGSHORN (P. Coronopus). - Otterbourne Hill.

GOOD KING HENRY (Chenopodium Bonus-Henricus).

GOOSEFOOT (C. album).

(C. urbicum).

DOCK (Rumex sanguineus).

(R. obtusfolius).

(R. pratensis).

WATER DOCK (R. Hydrolapathum). - Fit table-cloth for the butterfly's table.

SORREL (R. Acetosa).

LESSER SORREL (R. Acetosella). - Elegant and slender, making red clouds all over Cranbury.

BUCKWHEAT (Polygonum fagopyrum). - For several seasons in a meadow by Brooklyn. Now vanished.

KNOTGRASS (P. Convolvulus).

BLACK BINDWEED (P. aviculare).

WATER PEPPER (P. Hydropiper).

PERSICARIA (P. Persicaria).

(P. dumetorum). - Ampfield.

BASTARD TOADFLAX (Thesium linophyllum). - Crab Wood.

SUN SPURGE (Euphorbia Helioscopia). - Corn-fields.

WOOD S. (E. amygdaloides). - Cranbury and Otterbourne Park.

SMALL S. (E. Peplus).

(E. exigua).

DOG'S MERCURY (Mercurialis perennis). - First to clothe the banks with fresh vernal green.

NETTLE (Urtica dioica).

SMALL NETTLE (U. nana).

HOD (Humulus Lupulus). - If not native, it has taken well to the hedges, and clothes them with graceful wreaths.

ELM (Ulmus campestris) - Largest of spreading trees.

OAK (Quercus Robur). - Acorns differ on many trees. Five varieties of Cynips produce different oak-apples. Oak is still worn on the 29th of May, and it is called Shik-shak Day. Why?

BEECH (Fagus sylvatica). - Beautiful at Ampfield and South Lynch, and permitting only a select few plants to grow under its shade.

HAZEL (Corylus Avellana).

ALDER (Alnus glutinosa).

BIRCH (Betula alba). - Silver-leaved and white-barked, making fairy groves.

ASPEN (Populus tremula). - Aps, the people call it. The catkins are like caterpillars.

WILLOW or WITHY (Salix Caprea). - Our yellow goslings in spring, as they shoot from their silver rabbit-tail catkins, and our palms on Palm Sunday, though it is unlucky to bring one home earlier.

(S. triandra). - Near the old church, Otterbourne.

(S. rubra).

ROUND-LEAVED W. (S. aurita).

SALLOW W. (S. cinerea).

WHITE W. (S. alba).

(S. fragilis).

DWARF W. (S. repens). - Bogs towards Baddesley.

OSIER W. (S. viminalis). - Ampfield.

JUNIPER (Juniperus communis). - Above Standon on Down.

YEW (Taxus baccata). - Scattered in hedges, or singly all over the chalk district.

REEDMACE (Typha latifolia). - Itchen. Noble plant, commonly, but incorrectly, called bulrush.

BUR-REED (Sparganium ramosum). - With fertile flowers like prickly balls.

LORDS-AND-LADIES or CUCKOO-PINT (Arum maculatum). - Showing their heads under every hedge. The lords have a red column, the ladies a white.

DUCKWEED (Lemna trisulca).

GREAT WATER PLANTAIN (Alisma Plantago). - Stately ornament of bogs.

THE LILY TRIBE

GARLIC (Allium ursinum). - On road to Baddesley.

CROW G. (A. vineale). - Chalk ridges, if not destroyed by waterworks.

FLAG (Iris pseudacorus). - Itchen banks.

STINKING F. (I. fætidissima). - Not common, but in two copses, one at Cranbury and the other on the north of King's Lane.

DAFFODIL (Narcissus Pseudonarcissus). - Dell Copse, which it covers with the glory of the "dancing daffodil"; also plantation near Romsey Road.

BLACK BRYONY (Tamus communis). - Wreaths of shiny leaves.

SOLOMON'S SEAL (Polygonatum multiflorum). - Cranbury Wood.

BUTCHER'S BROOM (Ruscus aculeatus). - Otterbourne Hill.

BLUEBELL (Hyacinthus nonscriptus). - Masses in the woods.

WOODRUSH (Luzula sylvatica). - Graceful brown blossoms.

PYRAMIDAL ORCHIS (Orchis pyramidalis). - Chalk-pit by Sparrow Grove.

FOOL'S O. (O. Morio). - Cranbury.

PURPLE O. (O. mascula). - Local name, Dead Man's Fingers.

ROMSEY O. (O. incarnata). - Itchen meadows.

BROAD-LEAVED O. (O. latifolia). - Itchen meadows.

SPOTTED O. (O maculata).

DWARF O. (O. ustulata). - Downs by South Lynch.

SWEET O. (Gymnadenia conopsea). - Itchen meadows.

BUTTERFLY O. (Habenaria bifolia). - Sparrow Grove.

BEE O. (Ophrys apifera). - Railway banks and South Lynch.

FLY O. (O. muscifera). - South Lynch Down.

LADY'S TRESSES (Spiranthes autumnalis). - Cranbury lawn, but fitful in appearing.

TWAYBLADE (Listera ovata). - In hedges and woods.

BIRD'S-NEST ORCHIS (L. Nidus-avis). - Only under beeches.

HELLEBORINE (Epipactis latifolia). - Here and there in hedges.

(E. grandiflora). - Under beeches.

(E. palustris). - Chalk-pit.

REEDS

BOGRUSH (L. campestris). - Little rush.

(L. pilosa). - Ampfield Wood.

RUSH (Juncus conglomeratus). - The days of rush-lights are gone by, but rush-baskets for flowers and helmets are made by the children, and the white pith, when pressed, is made up into devices.

(F. effusus)

(F. glaucus) All in Itchen meadows.

(F. acutiflorus)

(F. squamosus)

BEAKRUSH (Rhynchospora fusca).

SINGLE BULRUSH (Scirpus lacustris).

(S. sylvatica). - Marsh near Baddesley Road.

(S. setaceus).

COTTON GRASS (Eriophorum angustifolium). - The soft cottony or silky heads are beautiful on the Itchen roads.

SEDGES (Carex pulicaris).

(C. acuta). - Copses.

(C. paniculata). - Itchen Canal.
(C. riparia). - Dell Copse.
STAR SEDGE (C. stellulata). - Copses.
(C. verna).
(C. acuta). - A lovely black and yellow fringe to the Itchen Canal.
(C. pallescens). - Damp places.
(C. paludosa). - Banks of Itchen Canal.
(C. sylvatica). - Cranbury.
(C. remota). - Boyatt Lane.
GRASSES
SWEET MEADOW GRASS (Anthoxanthum odoratum).
CANARY G. (Phalaris canariensis). - A stray.
FOXTAIL G. (Alopecurus pratensis).
(A. agrestis).
(A. geniculatus).
CAT-TAIL G. (Phleum pratense).
DOG'S G. (Agrostis canina).
(A. alba).
(A. vulgaris).
REED (Arundo Phragmites). - Waving brown tassels, beautiful for adornments - Itchen banks, and hedge of allotments on Otterbourne Hill.
MILLET GRASS (Milium effusum).
HAIR G. (Aira flexuosa).
(A. æspitosa). - Tufts on the hill, Otterbourne.
WILD OATS (Avena fatua). - Grown far more common than formerly.
(A. strigosa).
(A. pratensis).
(A. flavescens).
SOFT GRASS (Holcus mollis).
MELICK (Melica cærulea). - Cranbury.
(M. uniflora). - Dell Copse.
WHORL GRASS (Catabrosa aquatica). - The moat, Otterbourne.

(Glyceria nutans). - The moat.

MEADOW G. (Poa rigida).

(P. annua).

(P. nemoralis).

(P. pratensis).

(P. trivialis).

QUAKER'S G. (Briza media).

(B. minor).

DOG'S-TAIL G. (Cynosurus cristatus).

COCK'S-FOOT G. (Dactylis glomerata).

FESCUE (Festuca ovina).

(F. pratensis).

(F. lolacea).

BROME GRASS (Bromus giganteus). - Cranbury.

(B. asper).

(B. sterilis).

(B. racemosus).

(B. mollis).

(B. arvensis).

COUCH G. (Triticum caninum).

(T. repens).

RYE G. or MOUSE BARLEY (Lolium perenne). - Also Darnel.

FERNS, ETC.

BRACKEN (Pteris aquilina). - All over Cranbury.

HARD FERN (Blechnum boreale). - Mallibar Road between Albrook and Highbridge.

WALL-RUE (Asplenium Ruta-muraria).

BLACK MAIDENHAIR (A. Trichomanes). - Used to be on tombstones in old churchyard, Otterbourne.

LADY FERN (Athyrium Filix fæmina). - Cranbury.

(Ceterach officinale). - Merdon Castle.

HART'S TONGUE (Scolopendrium officinale).

(Polystichum angulare). - Cranbury.

MALE FERN (Lastrea Filix-mas).

(L. spinulosa).

(L. dilatata). - Otterbourne Park.

(L. thalipteris). - Cranbury.

HAY F. (L. Oreopteris). - Road to Baddesley.

POLYPODY (Polypodium vulgare).

ADDER'S TONGUE (Ophioglossum vulgare). - Field called Pleasure Grounds, Otterbourne.

HORSETAILS (Equisetum arvense).

(E. maximum).